hello midnight

Insomnia is when both sides of the pillow feel hot. —Anna Akhmatova

hello

Deborah Bishop and **David Levy**

A Touchstone Book

Published by Simon & Schuster

New York • London • Toronto • Sydney •Singapore

midnight

an **insomniac's** literary

bedside **companion**

TOUCHSTONE
Rockefeller Center
1230 Avenue of the Americas
New York, NY 10020

TOUCHSTONE and colophon are registered trademarks
of Simon & Schuster, Inc.

Permissions appear on pages 234–239.

Designed by Roger Gorman/Reiner NYC

Manufactured in the United States of America

10 9 8 7 6 5 4 3 2 1

Library of Congress Cataloging-in-Publication Data
Bishop, Deborah
    Hello midnight : an insomniac's literary bedside
    companion / Deborah Bishop and David Levy
        p. cm.
    Includes bibliographical references.
    1. Insomnia—Miscellanea. I. Levy, David. II. Title.
RC548.B57 2000
00-031717
ISBN 0-684-84834-1

To Michael, for giving me my sleep back.
—db

To my father and my sister. Rest in peace.
—dl

The authors would also like to thank the following folks for their interest in the project and subsequent suggestions: Jim Dorsey, Bob Glück, Julie Goldberg, Bill Hayes, Maggie Lake, Lois Nesbitt, Eugene Ostashevsky, Jonathan Polansky, Daniel Potter, Steven Sassaman, Tarin Towers, and Tom Wolferman.

contents

The woods are lovely, dark, and deep.

But I have promises to keep,

And miles to go before I sleep,

And miles to go before I sleep.

–Robert Frost

eyes
wide open

Five billion people go through the cycle of sleep and wakefulness every day, and relatively few of them know the joy of being fully rested and fully alert all day long.

—William Dement

an introduction

Dr. Dement, the father of modern sleep research, also asserted that "there were no sleep disorders before 1970," by which he meant that there were plenty of troubled sleepers, but little medical interest in their plight. In all of *The Interpretation of Dreams*, Freud's six-hundred-plus-page opus, for example, the subject of insomnia receives only a couple of passing footnotes.

Scientific concern about sleeplessness may be recent (the American Medical Association didn't recognize sleep medicine as a specialty until 1996), but there is nothing new about the condition—or its symptoms of dread, longing, reverie, and resignation. As we researched this book, one thing became clear: For better or worse, humankind is evolving into a community of the waking wounded, for whom a good night's sleep can be as elusive as a winning lottery ticket.

Cultural theorist Maurice Blanchot argues that insomnia is actually the last frontier of imagination and individual freedom. By defying sleep, he asserts, we resist the expectation that we will wake up rested, alert, and productive members of the social order. Indeed, there is evidence on these pages that insomnia may help transform some people into imaginative iconoclasts. But still, it is far more likely to spawn anxiety, despair, and distraction.

In our current culture of wakefulness, the enemies of sleep lurk everywhere. Outside, there is a Greek chorus of car alarms and boom boxes, a neighbor's muffled footsteps, the barking of a lonely dog, the distant laughter of midnight revelers (all of whom are having more fun than you); inside, there is the internal racket of your brain as it plays deejay to your top twenty fears, regrets, slights, and mortifications. As all insomniacs know, three in the morning sparks the dark side of the imagination, which hovers over past, present, and future terrors like a vulture scoping out its carrion.

For those who drop off to sleep with the toothpaste still fresh in their mouths, all of this is alien. Indeed, the world is divided into those who sleep well and everyone else—which happens to be the genesis of this book. After three wakeful nights, driven to distraction by jet lag, a premature midlife crisis, and the decibel level of a Manhattan summer, Deborah Bishop sat bemoaning her malady in an East Village bar with David Levy, a New Yorker who has no trouble sleeping in the city that doesn't. She clutched her hair, he rolled his eyes—and together they decided to tackle the topic from both sides.

For those of you seeking a cure, bookstore shelves groan with self-help guides, drugstores beckon with bottles full of hope, and sleep clinics seduce with the latest medical advances. This collection of facts, insights, quips, and laments offers something different: Amusement. Distraction. A reason to divert your gaze (or that of a sleepless friend) from the leer of the bedside clock. And the pleasure of knowing that, in your wide-eyed state, you're in very good company, a member of a club that includes geniuses, statesmen, musicians, movie stars, authors, scientists, wits, and one of your humble authors.

Deborah Bishop
David Asher Levy
November 1999

A bad night lies ahead
And a new day beyond that—
A simple sequence, but hard
To remember in the right order.

—Mark Jarman, "Psalm: The New Day"

nights

of the

living

dead

An Epidemic with No Vaccine

Number of modern-day Americans who "have trouble" sleeping:

100,00

The Epidemic in Facts and Figures

Rank of sleep disorders among undiagnosed and untreated medical problems in America: 1

Percentage decline in Americans' average nightly sleep in the twentieth century: 20

Percentage of Americans who don't get their recommended eight hours of nightly sleep: 66

Percentage of those who get less than six hours nightly: 33

Percentage of people who "function well" on less than six hours of sleep: 5

Number who suffer from potentially fatal disorders such as sleep apnea and narcolepsy: 20 million

Number of individual sleep disorders defined by modern research: 82

Percentage of Americans who report that sleep deprivation affects their work: 66

Corresponding yearly loss in productivity: $70 billion

Car crashes per year in the U.S. blamed on sleepy drivers: 200,000

Yearly domestic death toll from accidents caused by sleeplessness: 24,000

Ratio of women to men who seek medical help for sleeplessness: 2 to 1

Percentage of those not seeking medical advice who self-medicate with drugs, alcohol, or over-the-counter remedies: 40

Number of years the average seventy-six-year-old will have spent asleep: 23

Number of years the average seventy-six-year-old will have spent dreaming: 5.5

Number of sleep-disorder clinics accredited by the American Sleep Disorders Association in 1987: 92

Number accredited in 1997: 365

Number of nonaccredited sleep-disorder clinics in 1999: 2,600

Common price for an overnight stay at a sleep clinic in 1999: $1,500

The lion and the calf shall lie down together,
but the calf won't get much sleep.

—Woody Allen

Asleep at the Wheel

The supertanker *Exxon Valdez* barrels into an Alaskan reef, fouling miles of coastline with its cargo of crude oil. The space shuttle *Challenger* explodes moments after takeoff, incinerating the crew and tarnishing the entire U.S. space program. A nuclear accident at Three Mile Island threatens to transform the surrounding area into a radioactive wasteland.

After the expensive investigations are over and the tower of reports is published, these disasters are inevitably attributed to "human error." But the headlines make little of the abundant evidence that—in these and other daily mishaps, large and small—the errors were caused by lack of sleep.

The National Transportation Safety Board concluded that "the cause of the [*Valdez*] grounding . . . was the failure of the third mate to maneuver the vessel because . . . he was asleep on his feet." The commission investigating the *Challenger* disaster found that two of the three top project managers had slept less than three hours apiece for three consecutive nights before the launch. And the Three Mile Island emergency began at four A.M., when graveyard-shift workers missed a mechanical failure.

Even if you don't pilot an oil tanker or a spacecraft, as an insomniac you're likely to be more accident prone. Some experts estimate that driving while fatigued leads to as many as half of all fatal accidents on the road, making it even more life threatening than drunk driving. Alas, there is no known remedy except getting ample sleep—and keeping an eye peeled for that drowsy guy sailing through the stop sign.

Laughing, with a TV's blue-static figures
        dancing through the air at 2 A.M.
with eight empty beer bottles lined up
        on the kitchen table, a full moon
gazing through the opened back door,
        his thick fingers drumming the pink
laminex, singing along with a rock video
        of soft porno, recounting dead friends,
with a tally of all his mistakes
        in front of him, after he's punched
the walls & refrigerator with his fist,
        unable to forget childhood's lonely
grass & nameless flowers & insects,
        crying for his black cat
hit by a car, drawing absent faces
        on the air with right index finger,
rethinking lost years of a broken marriage
        like a wrecked ship inside a green bottle,
puffing a horn-shaped ceramic pipe,
        dragging his feet across the floor
in a dance with the shadow of a tree
        on a yellow wall, going to the wooden fence
to piss under the sky's marsupial stare,
        walking back in to pop the cap
on his last beer, hugging himself awake,
        picking up a dried wishbone
from the table & snapping it, cursing the world,
        softly whispering his daughter's name,
he disturbs the void that is
        heavy as the heart's clumsy logbook.

—Yusef Komunyakaa, "When Loneliness Is a Man"

It is no
small art
to sleep:
to achieve
it one
must keep
awake
all day.

—Friedrich Nietzsche

The Hormone Perplex

Decades after scientists had solved most of the mysteries about sleep—like how it functions and why it sometimes fails—one big question remained: *Why on earth do we do it?*

That is, until recently. Researchers are now discovering that sleep is the only state in which crucial hormone levels are monitored by our bodies and reset to cope with the stresses of waking life. Lose sleep, and your body loses control of its hormonal balance, threatening to make you sick, overweight, and old before your time.

Eve Van Cauter, a researcher at the University of Chicago, took round-the-clock blood samples from volunteers while they were awake and then as they slept. She found that when people cheat on sleep, they show rising levels of the stress hormone cortisol in their blood. Cortisol, released by the adrenal glands, is the chemical agent that induces "fight or flight" behavior—the acute sharpening of your senses when confronted with conflict or danger. This potent hormone is helpful when you encounter a grizzly bear at your campsite, but it isn't meant to roil through your blood for extended periods of time. Studies show that long-term exposure to high levels of cortisol can shrink the hippocampus, a critical region of the brain that regulates learning and memory. Furthermore, as cortisol rises in the sleep-deprived, the levels of two other hormones—human growth hormone, which builds muscle, and prolactin, which oversees the immune system—plummet.

All of these hormone levels are checked and tweaked only in the deepest delta phase of sleep—a phase that normally begins to dwindle in frequency and duration between the ages of thirty-five and forty-five. So, lose sleep in your youth, and you essentially accelerate the aging process.

Ironic, indeed, that the very quest for youth, beauty, and power demanded by our work-hard, play-hard culture is slowly depriving us of the things we value most.

Twenty minutes past
four, sharp,
and here's Baby
wide-eyed as a
marigold ...
This is what brings
about hatred and
bloodshed,
that's what *this* does.

—Dorothy Parker

Hands on a Hard Body

directed by
S. R. Bindler (1998)

The tongue-in-cheek title implies pornography, but the body in question is that of a shiny new pickup, and the only lust displayed is for possession of this free truck. In order to win a competition sponsored by a Texas dealership, contestants simply must stand there, with at least one hand on the truck—until only one person is left standing. This modern-day dance marathon pits two dozen people against each other, themselves, and their own sleep-deprived brains. The resulting documentary works on many levels. It's a study of oddball characters, a meditation on the mind/body relationship, and a fascinating slice of Americana.

insomnia

by Stephen King

"People die from lack of sleep all the time," Wyzer was saying, **"although the medical examiner usually ends up writing** *suicide* **on the cause-of-death line, rather than** *insomnia.* **Insomnia and alcoholism have a lot in common, but the major thing is this: they're both diseases of the heart and mind, and when they're allowed to run their course they usually gut the spirit long before they're able to destroy the body. So yeah—people** *do* **die from lack of sleep."**

Ralph Roberts has had a rough year. Ever since his beloved wife, Carolyn, succumbed to cancer, Ralph has been waking up earlier and earlier, exhausted yet entirely unable to fall back asleep.

Ralph's friends and neighbors offer sure-fire cures ranging from exercise and acupuncture to chamomile tea, whiskey, brandy, music, chiropractic, and magic crystals, to no avail. As Ralph's wake-up time creeps closer to two A.M., he begins to see the world in a new light (and as Stephen King fans

already know, the light in Derry, Maine, is never friendly)——one that resembles the disoriented, hallucinatory state of the sleep deprived. Sleepless Ralph starts seeing things that aren't there—or, to be more precise, he begins to see things that have always been there, invisible to the rested. His visions include strange auras that reveal other people's states of mind; through the auras, kindly neighbors are transformed into wife beaters and murderers, three little bald doctors become death brokers who inhabit the homes of the terminally ill. Ralph's demonic visions are visible only to those who share his affliction.

To anyone who has ever lain alert while the world sleeps, Ralph's wakefulness and brief bouts of false hope will feel all too familiar:

His eyelids were so heavy they felt as if they had been dipped in concrete, and although he was reading the tennis article carefully, word for word, he had no idea of what the writer was driving at. Whole sentences zipped across his brain without sticking, like cosmic rays.

I'm going to sleep tonight—I really think I am. For the first time in months the sun is going to have to come up without my help, and that isn't just good, friends and neighbors; that is great.

Then, shortly after three o'clock, that pleasant drowsiness began to disappear. It did not go with a champagne-cork pop but rather seemed to ooze away, like sand through a fine sieve or water down a partially clogged drain. When Ralph realized what was happening, it wasn't panic he felt, but a sick dismay. It was a feeling he had come to recognize as the true opposite of hope, and when he slipper-scuffed his way into the bedroom at quarter past three, he couldn't remember a depression as deep as the one which now enveloped him. He felt as if he were suffocating in it.

"Please, God, just forty winks," he muttered as he turned off the light, but he strongly suspected that this was one prayer which was not going to be answered.... Sleep, that undiscriminating friend, humankind's best and most reliable nurse since the dawn of time, had abandoned him again.

pillow

The Few, the Proud, the Sleepless

pride and prejudice

Only dolts and drudges sleep.

—Isak Dinesen, "Night Walk"

When you lie awake in the wee hours, with no company but your own consciousness, there is one bright spot in the darkness: here is proof that you are, indeed, special.

Joyce Carol Oates wrote of "the secret pride of the insomniac who, for all his anguish, for all his very real discomfort, knows himself set apart from all the others." "Dearest friends," groused the sleepless Dorothy Parker, "A sweet lot of dearest friends *I've* got. All of them lying in swinish stupors, while I'm practically up and about. All of them stretched sodden through these, the fairest hours of the day, when man should be at his most productive." Perhaps with people like Parker in mind, Dr. Henry Kellerman of New York's Postgraduate Center for Mental Health theorizes that many insomniacs nourish a "highly critical attitude . . . the main emotion [of which is their] underlying anger at the imperfections in the world."

Certainly, if you find yourself night after night staring at the ceiling, it becomes tempting to view the slumbering masses as complacent, cowlike—and worthy of contempt. As the insomniac novelist Vladimir Nabokov sneered "Sleep is the most moronic fraternity in the world, with the heaviest dues and crudest rituals,"

Men who are unhappy,
like men who sleep badly,
are always proud of the
fact.

—Bertrand Russell

All my life I have been a poor go-to-sleeper. People in trains, who lay their newspaper aside, fold their silly arms, and immediately, with an offensive familiarity of demeanor, start snoring, amaze me as much as the uninhibited chap who cozily defecates in the presence of a chatty tubber. . . . [Sleep] is a mental torture I find debasing. The strain and drain of composition

The Novelist's
Nightmare

often force me, alas, to swallow a strong pill that gives me an hour or two of frightful nightmares or even to accept the comic relief of a midday snooze, the way a senile rake might totter to the nearest euthanasium; but I simply cannot get used to the nightly betrayal of reason, humanity, genius. No matter how great my weariness, the wrench of parting with consciousness is unspeakably repulsive to me.

—Vladimir Nabokov, *Speak, Memory*

Sleep is such a dull, stupid state of existence that even amongst mere animals we despise them most which are most drowsy. —William Law, *A Serious Call to a Devout and Holy Life* (1728)

In my opinion, sleep is a habit, acquired by the environment. Like all habits it is generally carried to extremes. The man that sleeps four hours soundly is better off than a dreamy sleeper of eight hours. —Thomas Edison

Six hours of sleep for a man, seven for a woman, eight for a fool. —Victorian Proverb

I'll sleep when I'm dead. —Warren Zevon

The Princess and the Pea

by Hans Christian Andersen

In the morning the queen asked her,

"Did you sleep well?"

"Oh, terribly badly!" said the princess. "I hardly closed my eyes all night."

So, this prince has been wandering the world looking for a suitable wife, but there's something wrong with all the women he meets: they're just not *perfect* enough. (This man has since become an archetype of pop psychology, but that's another story.)

When a potential SWP (single white princess) shows up at the palace in a full-force gale, with rain streaming down her hair and leaking out of her shoes, the queen devises a litmus test. Placing a single pea on a bare bedstead, she then piles on twenty mattresses and twenty feather beds. After retiring, the maiden tosses and turns all night, and not because of a fear of heights: "Heaven knows what was in the bed," she complains. "I seemed to be lying on something very hard, and this morning my whole body is black and blue."

Since no one but a real princess could possibly have such finely honed sensibilities, the prince's bachelor days are ended by a royal bout of legume-induced insomnia.

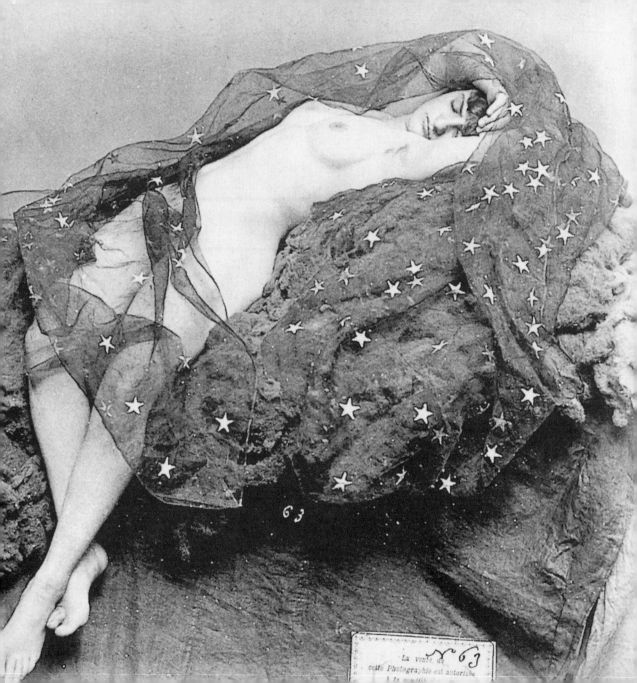

wool
gathering

1,345 SHEEP AND STILL COUNTING . . .

I really can't be expected
to drop everything and start
counting sheep at my age.
I hate sheep.

—Dorothy Parker, "The Little Hours"

Counting sheep combines two self-hypnosis techniques: the visualization of a peaceful scene and the mantra-like repetition of numbers. But do people really fall asleep while tallying lambs? And how did this tireless advice arise? Long ago, perhaps some shepherd was lulled by his companions' placid stares; leaping sheep have been woven into the cultural fabric ever since.

One thing's for certain: for Romantic poets like William Wordsworth and urban wits like Dorothy Parker, sheep lag far behind Seconal and alcohol in their ability to inspire slumber.

A flock of sheep that leisurely pass by
One after one; the sound of rain and bees
Murmuring; the fall of rivers, winds and seas,
Smooth fields, white sheets of water, and pure sky;
I've thought of all by turns, and still I lie
Sleepless . . .

—William Wordsworth, "To Sleep"

The absurd device of counting
for preventing you from

Untender it may be in me, but all my life I've hated sheep. It amounts to a phobia, the way I hate them. I can tell the minute there's one in the room. They needn't think that I am going to lie here in the dark and count their unpleasant little faces for them; I wouldn't do it if I didn't fall asleep again until the middle of next August.... Let them count themselves, if they're so crazy mad after mathematics. Let them do their own dirty work. Coming around here, at this time of day, and asking me to count them! —Dorothy Parker, "The Little Hours"

When Violet can't
she doesn't
she counts

heep is merely a transparent ruse
hinking about anything important.
-Quentin Crisp

Everything began to be better for Mrs. Reinhardt from the moment she started to sleep-walk. Every night her journey yielded a fresh surprise. First it was that she saw sheep—not sheep as one sees them in life, a bit sooty and bleating away, but sheep as one sees them in a dream. She saw myriads of white fleece on a hilltop, surrounded by little lambs frisking and suckling to their hearts' content. —Edna O'Brien, "Number 10"

sleep
count sheep,
men. —Frank Capra, notes for *It's a Wonderful Life*

to sleep, perchance to die

perchance to die

The Fine Line Between a Little Snooze and the Big Sleep

SHE WAS NOT ALIVE...NOR DEAD...

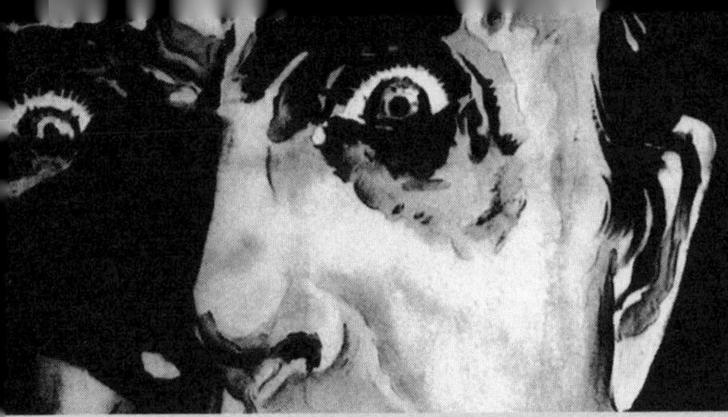

I had been living for a long time with the knowledge that if I ever shut my eyes in the dark and let myself go, my soul would go out of my body.

—Ernest Hemingway, "Now I Lay Me"

Sleep . . . Oh! how I loathe those little slices of death . . . —Henry Wadsworth Longfellow

When the Greek poet Homer wrote that "sleep is the twin of death," he meant it quite literally. In Greek mythology, the goddess Night bore twin sons (the father remains a mystery) whom she named Hypnos and Thanatos—Sleep and Death. Hypnos, pal to mortals, roamed the earth in several guises: a child, a bird, and a youth ministering to man's health and happiness with a sleep-inducing poppy potion. Thanatos, his spiteful twin, hated all men.

Insomniacs through the years have fretted over the vexing connection between these twin gods. Franz Kafka, after consecutive sleepless nights alone in his Prague garret, confided to his diary, "Perhaps my insomnia only conceals a great fear of death. Perhaps I am afraid the soul—which in sleep leaves me—will never return."

The thought of suicide has gotten me through many a sleepless night. —Friedrich Nietzsche

1,001 (Sleepless) Nights

Some insomniacs may equate the abandonment of consciousness with death, the "Big Sleep."

But for the fabled storyteller Scheherazade, staying up all night yakking was the only way to stay her execution.

For three years, King Shahriyar had been ravishing virgins and then beheading them in the morning, as revenge for his wife's adultery. When there were no maidens left but the daughters of his own counselor, the eldest girl, Scheherazade, nobly volunteered to go. But she escaped her gruesome fate by entertaining the king with a new tale each night, stopping every time at an especially interesting point. After 1,001 nights of her stories, the king declared himself a changed man. Scheherazade got to keep her head—and became his queen.

When I lie awake at night, afraid that I am walking through the valley of the shadow of death, I feel that I am still the entangled Brooklyn boy who all his life has depended on his will. And there I am in the terrors of the night, still trying to . . . outwit death.

—Alfred Kazin, *A Lifetime Burning in Every Moment*

We term sleep a death; and yet it is waking that kills us, and destroys those spirits that are the house of life.

—Sir Thomas Browne, *Religio Medici*

Let's just say that you do fall asleep at a normal hour. Then the odds are that you will wake up at four in the morning, having dreamed that you have died. [And] death turns out to feel much more frantic than you had imagined.

—Anne Lamott, *Bird by Bird*

I work all day, and get half-drunk at night.
Waking at four to soundless dark, I stare.
In time the curtain-edges will grow light.
Till then I see what's really always there:
Unresting death, a whole day nearer now,
Making all thought impossible but how
And where and when I shall myself die.
Arid interrogation: yet the dread
Of dying, and being dead,
Flashes afresh to hold and horrify.

—Philip Larkin, "Aubade"

And each day dies with sleep.

—Gerard Manley Hopkins

Sleep's but a short death; death's but a longer sleep.

—Phineas Fletcher, *The Locusts*

If I should die before I wake, I pray the Lord my soul to take.

—Child's bedtime prayer

The Insomniac's
Film Festival

Brother of Sleep (Schlafes Bruder)

directed by

Joseph Vilsmaier (1995)

Born in a remote mountain village in early-nineteenth-century Austria, Elias Adler is a poster boy for oversensitivity. His ears are so perceptive that he can hear the most subtle sounds; his love for a neighbor's daughter is so strong that he cannot bring himself to consummate it. Music becomes his refuge, but his obvious genius for it provides both solace and affliction. Eventually, his oddness causes the villagers to shun him and the object of his affection to marry another man. Wounded in heart and soul, Adler decides to end his life in a novel way—by not sleeping anymore. He dies as he lived, suffering from a fatal acuity of consciousness.

behind
twitching eyes

The Mystical State of REM

Some must watch while some mu\[

The next time you're lying awake next to a dozing bedmate, try this: Watch the eyes until the lids begin to quiver. Wait a few minutes, then "accidentally" wake your paramour in midtwitch. The odds are good that, after snorting in protest, he or she will regale you with a graphically recalled dream—then roll over in an attempt to revive the subconscious vision you rudely interrupted (assuming, of course, it wasn't that recurring nightmare about showing up for the final exam late, naked, and at the wrong building).

Scientists first posited a connection between rapid eye movement (REM) and dreaming more than a century ago, but it wasn't until 1953 (the same year that the structure of DNA was discovered) that a graduate- and dental-school dropout named Eugene Aserinsky thought to wire his dozing son to an electroencephalograph (EEG) to study the physiology behind sleepers' fluttering eyes. When the EEG went wild with brainwave activity corresponding to his eight-year-old's eye movements, Aserinsky— who'd been taken in by sleep-research pioneer Nathaniel Kleitman at the University of Chicago—stumbled on a major discovery and entered the annals of science, albeit by the back door. After repeating the experiment hundreds of times in controlled laboratory conditions with a variety of subjects, Aserinsky, Kleitman, and William Dement, another distinguished sleep researcher, proved that sleep was

—Shakespeare, *Hamlet*

not a monolithic state of unconsciousness, but a complex world of five distinct phases, including REM. This discovery set the cornerstone for all succeeding sleep research, and eventually brought the term REM into common parlance: witness the popular rock band, whose lyrics drip with dream imagery.

> **If sleep does not serve an absolutely vital function, then it is the biggest mistake the evolutionary process ever made.**
>
> —Dr. Allan Rechtschaffen, University of Chicago

Intriguingly, REM follows the deepest stage of sleep, yet its brainwave patterns are extremely similar to those recorded during wakefulness. During REM sleep, muscle twitching is abundant, yet spinal reflexes are absent—the body is essentially unable to act out the dreams being experienced. REM sleep seems to have a restorative effect on the tired mind and body, yet oxygen consumption, blood flow to the brain, and heart and respiration rates are often greater during REM than when we're awake—physiologically, its effects are similar to intense emotional agitation.

REM sleep (or the lack of it) is such an alluring mystery that it is still being actively investigated today, especially as a factor in all sorts of sleep disorders, including insomnia.

Kittens on the Verge of a Nervous Breakdown

Every parent knows that infants dream a lot. Squirming, grimacing, clutching the air with tiny fists—babies' eyes twitch, deep in the REM phase, for eight to ten hours a day. (Fetuses in the womb are thought to dream virtually 'round the clock.) The emotional expressions and motor activity associated with dreaming—for instance, the "smile of the angels," a baby's grin—occur in REM sleep long before they do in wakefulness.

In 1966, three sleep researchers at Columbia University proposed that the sensory stimulus provided by dreams is essential for the health of the developing brain. An abundance of dreams, the theory goes, stimulates and fine-tunes an infant's central nervous system in the same way that physical exercise stimulates growing muscle tissue.

Unable to test the theory on human subjects, they conspired to prevent a group of newborn kittens from enjoying REM sleep. Many child-rearing gurus agree that premature disruptions in a baby's natural sleep patterns can lead to stress, anxiety, and insomnia in later life, and the dream-deprived kittens did, indeed, display some noticeable disruptions in their youthful brains. Whether or not they grew up to be well-adjusted members of the feline community is not a matter of scientific record.

Slaves to the Switch

The biochemical switch that prevents your brain from controlling your muscles during REM sleep plays a crucial role in your personal safety. Without it, your dreaming brain might command your body to flay enemies, fly out of windows, or flee dragons. Sleepwalking, -talking, and -eating are symptoms of a malfunctioning switch. In severe cases, called "night terrors," dreamers act out their worst nightmares, occasionally doing violence to themselves and others. (One man in Scotland, for example, was acquitted of killing his wife during a night terror, because the jury believed that he was not fully conscious of his actions.) Conversely, if the switch fails to turn on when you wake, you may find yourself momentarily paralyzed—thinking of coffee but quite unable to brew it.

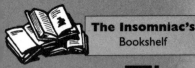

The House of Sleep

by Jonathan Coe

The next morning, Terry awoke.

An ordinary enough event in the lives of most people, perhaps: but not for him. The sensation of passing from sleep to wakefulness had eluded Terry for more than a decade, and although today he was at least aware, as soon as dawn began to glimmer around the edges of his bedroom's small, thickly curtained window, that something new and exceptional had taken place.

Written in sections that mirror the five stages of sleep, Coe's dreamlike novel shifts back and forth in time as it follows the adventures, relationships, and various sleep disorders of four characters who first meet at Ashdown, a fortress-like university residence hall looming over the English coast.

Sarah is a student teacher and undiagnosed narcoleptic whose vividly detailed dreams are indistinguishable from reality. Her first boyfriend, Gregory, is a cold and manipulative medical researcher who goes off to London to pursue his career. Soon after, Sarah has a fleeting flirtation and strange friendship with Robert, a fragile and hesitant young man who is unable to forget her in the ensuing years. Robert's best friend Terry is a film-obsessed misanthrope who sleeps fourteen hours a day and wakes only with the greatest reluctance—unwilling to break away from his dreams "of near-paradisal loveliness; dreams of sun-dappled gardens, heavenly vistas, ambrosial picnics and perfect sexual encounters ..."

A decade later Terry has become a caffeine-fueled journalist and medical anomaly who barely needs to sleep at all. Curious to return to the visions of his youth he finds himself once again at Ashdown, which has since been converted into a sleep disorders clinic directed by the increasingly deranged Gregory, who is determined to find a cure for sleep—by any means:

"I'll tell you why: because the sleeper is helpless; powerless. Sleep puts even the strongest people at the mercy of the weakest and most feeble. Can you imagine what it must be like for a woman of Mrs. Thatcher's fibre, her moral character, to be obliged to prostrate herself every day in that posture of abject submission? The brain disabled, the muscles inert and flaccid? It must be insupportable."

the hour of the

wolf

It's Dark, It's Cold, and Nobody Loves You

She feels crazier and more scared as dawn approaches, the moments between night and day, the hour of the wolf, the hour of the black dogs.

—Anne Lamott, *Rosie*

For those who hold no visa to the state of REM, minutes pass like hours and the night plays host to a hit parade of real fears and imaginary monsters, all distorted like reflections in a funhouse mirror. For most insomniacs, the freak show builds to a climax somewhere between three and five A.M.

During these hours that F. Scott Fitzgerald deemed "the real dark night of the soul," thoughts leapfrog like evil imps, hell-bent on destruction. Every silver lining has a cloud; no slight goes unforgotten. Before you eventually escape into sleep, this much you will know: Your life is a sham. You will die alone. Your beauty is spent. They were laughing *at* you, not with you. The night will never end. The night will end forever.

At three o'clock in the morning a forgotten package has the same tragic importance as a death sentence.

—F. Scott Fitzgerald, "Pasting It Together" (from *The Crack-Up*)

In the middle of the night you wake up. You start to cry.

What's happening to me? Oh, my life, oh my youth. . . .

There's some wine left in the bottle. You drink it.

The clock ticks. Sleep . . .

—Jean Rhys, *Good Morning Midnight*

...this is the zero hour.

This is the time the swooning soul hangs pendant and vertiginous between the new day and the old, nor dares confront the one or summon back the other. This is the time when all things, known and hidden, are iron to weight the spirit; when all ways, traveled or virgin, fall away from the stumbling feet, when all before the straining eyes is black. Blackness now, everywhere is blackness. This is the time of abomination, the dreadful hour of the victorious dark. For it is always darkest—Was it not that lovable old cynic, La Rochefoucauld, who said it is always darkest before the deluge? —Dorothy Parker, "The Little Hours"

Past midnight. Never knew such silence.

The earth might be uninhabited . . .

Perhaps my best years are gone . . .

But I wouldn't want them back.

Not with the fire in me now.

No, I wouldn't want them back.

—Samuel Beckett, *Krapp's Last Tape*

When you lie
down at night
turning from
side to side
and you can't
be satisfied
no way you do
Old Man Blues
got you

—Leadbelly

Four in the Morning

The hour from night to day.

The hour from side to side.

The hour for those past thirty.

The hour swept clean to the crowing of cocks.

The hour when earth betrays us.

The hour when wind blows from extinguished stars.

The hour of and-what-nothing-remains-after-us.

The hollow hour.

Blank, empty.

The very pit of all other hours.

No one feels good at four in the morning.

If ants feel good at four in the morning

three cheers for the ants. And let five o'clock come

if we are to go on living.

—Wisława Szymborska

It is always darkest
just before the day
dawneth.

—Thomas Fuller (1650)

Hours sleepless, deep in the night, when I go forth, speeding swiftly the country roads, or through the city streets, or pacing miles and miles, stifling plaintive cries.—Walt Whitman

No matter what time I go to sleep [I] wake and hear the clock strike either one or two then lie wide awake and hear three, four and five. But since I have stopped giving a good goddamn about anything in the past it doesn't bother [me] much and I lie there and keep perfectly still....The trouble is that if you start thinking about anything in that wakeing time you go all through it and exhaust it and are pooped in the morning when you have to write. If you can lie still and take it easy and not just consider your life and everything else as an outsider and *not give a damn*—it is a hell of a help. —Ernest Hemingway, letter to F. Scott Fitzgerald, 1935

Twice I woke up tonight and wandered to the window. And the lights down on the street, like pale omission points, tried to complete the fragment of a sentence spoken through sleep, but diminished into darkness, too.

—Joseph Brodsky, "On Love"

Hour of the Lamb (A Contrarian View)

The faithful have their imaginations well in hand. They do not lie awake at night imagining earthquakes, tornadoes, flash floods, or nuclear war. They do not entertain the possibility of being axed to death in their beds by a psychokiller on the loose from the psychiatric hospital on the eastern edge of town. They do not lie there wide-eyed for hours picturing malignant cells galloping through their uteruses, their intestines, their prostate glands, or their brains. To the faithful, a headache is a headache, not a brain tumor. They do not imagine themselves rotting away from the inside out. They do not have detailed sexual fantasies about the mailman, the aerobics instructor, or their children's Grade Two teacher. The nights of the faithful are peaceful. Even their nightmares have happy endings. The faithful wake up smiling. Their subconsciouses are clear.

—Diane Schoemperlen, *Forms of Devotion*

Now you hear what the house has to say.

Pipes clanking, water running in the dark,

the mortgaged walls shifting in discomfort,

and voices mounting in an endless drone

of small complaints like the sounds of a family

that year by year you've learned how to ignore.

But now you must listen to the things you own,

all that you've worked for these past years,

the murmur of property, of things in disrepair,

the moving parts about to come undone,

and twisting in the sheets remember all

the faces you could not bring yourself to love.

How many voices have escaped you until now,

the venting furnace, the floorboards underfoot,

the steady accusations of the clock

numbering the minutes no one will mark.

The terrible clarity this moment brings,

the useless insight, the unbroken dark.

—Dana Gioia, "Insomnia"

In the middle of the night, the terrible

middle of the night, I writhe sleepless in

a bed that is like a raft in a devouring

ocean. As I have all my life when I feel

myself up against the ropes, I pray to a

God who cannot be very real, since he

seems to be only a word, a name, a

hope, a reach. Yet I pray; it is suffocating

to be so bound up in oneself, a tangle of

longings, useless memories, and violent

recriminations.

—Alfred Kazin, *A Lifetime Burning in Every Moment*

Even when I fall asleep early,

My nights are long and full of bitterness.

Tonight, tortured with insomnia,

Memories of the past flood back

Until they have exhausted me.

Alone in the house beside a smoky lamp,

I rub my heavy eyelids

And idly turn the pages of my notebook.

Again and again I scratch my head

And trim my brush and stir the heavy ink.

The hours go by. The moon comes

And stands in the open door,

White and shining like molten silver.

Suddenly I am back, sailing on Ts'ai Fong River

With the fellows of my youth,

Back in Yuen village.

Oh wonderful mountains! Oh noble boys!

How is it that I have lived so long

And never once gone back to visit you?

—Lu Yu (1125–1209), "Insomnia"

Typically you'll try to comfort yourself by thinking about the day's work—the day's excrementitious work. You may experience a jittery form of existential dread, considering the absolute meaninglessness of life and the fact that no one has ever really loved you; you may find yourself consumed with a free-floating shame, and a hopelessness about your work, and the realization that you will have to throw out everything you've done so far and start from scratch. But you will not be able to do so. Because you suddenly understand that you are completely riddled with cancer. —Anne Lamott, *Bird by Bird*

The Crack-Up

by F. Scott Fitzgerald

It appears that every man's insomnia is as different from his neighbor's as are their daytime hopes and aspirations.

The author of *The Great Gatsby* devoted endless psychic energy to seeking the elusive Mr. Sandman, as documented in his essay collection *The Crack-Up.* In "Sleeping and Waking," he attributes his first serious bout of insomnia to a losing encounter with a mosquito: "It is astonishing how much worse one mosquito can be than a swarm. A swarm can be prepared against, but *one* mosquito takes on a personality—a hatefulness, a sinister quality of the struggle to the death."

After this episode, Fitzgerald became what he calls "sleep conscious," and the prospect of whether or not he would sleep through the night "began to haunt [him] long before bedtime." As with many insomniacs, Fitzgerald followed precise bedtime rituals in the hopes of encouraging sleep: He laid out a glass of water, extra pajamas, special pills, a notebook and a pencil; drank a nightcap; and chose a book over which to become drowsy: "So far so good. From midnight until two-thirty peace in the room. Then suddenly I am awake, harassed by one of the ills or functions of the body, a too vivid dream, a change in the weather for warm or cold.... The *real* night, the darkest hour, has begun."

The author's time-tested sleep remedies—fantasies of saving the day as a Princeton quarterback or a courageous war hero (neither of which he was ever in a position to actually do)—were eventually "worn thin with years of usage." What remains is recrimination and regret, described in the early-morning mantra:

I need not have hurt her like that.
Nor said this to him.
Nor broken myself trying to break what
**   was unbreakable ...**
I am a ghost now as the clock
**   strikes four ...**
Irresistible, iridescent—here is Aurora
**   —here is another day.**

# of an hour, one's own

Exploiting the Midnight Hour

I prefer the dark part of the night, after midnight and before four-thirty, when it's more bare, more hollow. Then I can breathe, and can think while others are sleeping, in a way can stop time, can have it so—this has always been my dream—so that while everyone else is frozen, I can work busily about them, doing whatever it is that needs to be done, like the elves who make the shoes while the children sleep.

—Dave Eggers, *A Heartbreaking Work of Staggering Genius*

These new poems of mine have one thing in common, they were all written at about four in the morning—that still blue, almost eternal hour before the baby's cry, before the glassy music of the milkman, settling his bottles.

—Sylvia Plath

Although most insomniacs feel themselves to be among the waking wounded, many have made peace with their condition and even regard it with affection. For some, especially women, the hour of the wolf is a precious, unshared time, free of the impositions that gather momentum after dawn. The poet Emily Dickinson, for example, wrote feverishly at night, sometimes scribbling right off the page as she battled with—then yielded to—sleep.

The critic A. Alvarez describes Sylvia Plath likewise composing the poems that appeared in her collection *Ariel* at a time when most people have the strength only to dream: "In those dead hours between night and day, she was able to gather herself in silence and isolation, almost as though she were reclaiming some past innocence and freedom before life got a grip on her. Then she could write. For the rest of the day she was shared among the children, the housework, the shopping, efficient, bustling, harassed, like every other housewife."

When Joyce Carol Oates's insomnia first dogged her in her adolescence, she appreciated the extra time to read and write: "Early on, the night became synonymous with imagination and freedom and solitude—everything you need to be creative—and so I've come to regard my insomnia as something very positive. I've written a lot of gothic and horror, and I think the insomnia allows me to tap into something that might otherwise be missing."

And doesn't a wakeful author deserve an equally alert audience? James Joyce thought so. In his challenging and monolithic work *Finnegans Wake*, Joyce describes "that ideal reader suffering from an ideal insomnia."

Yes. I think owing to the sudden rush of two wakeful nights, making up early mornings rather, I think I see the end of *Here & Now* [the novel later titled *The Years*].

—Virginia Woolf, diary entry, August 17, 1934

I have terrible nights of insomnia, when my mind is galloping along and I feel a strange eerie nervousness, absolutely inexplicable. What a nuisance! Or, maybe it isn't a nuisance? An ideal insomnia allows for a lot of reading. When the house is dark and quiet and the entire world turned off for the night, it's a marvelous feeling to be there alone, with a book, or a blank piece of paper. . . . Such moments of solitude redeem all the rushing hours, the daylight confusion of people and duties.

—Joyce Carol Oates

It was after supper that night—as usual a glass of milk and some bread and cheese—that it happened. My fingers tingled, and the palms of my hands. I pulled a chair up to the table, opened an exercise book, and wrote *This is my Diary.* But it wasn't a diary. I remembered everything that had happened to me in the last year and a half. I remembered what he'd said, what I'd felt. I wrote on until late into the night. . . .

The landlady was rather late bringing up my breakfast. She put the tray down and said, "I must tell you, miss, that the gentleman in the room below has complained about you. He says that you walked up and down all night. He thought he heard you crying and laughing. He couldn't get to sleep until three in the morning, and he says if it happens again he's going to leave . . ."

I got out of bed and said, "All right, I'll leave at the end of the week. But now you must get out." I took her by the shoulders and pushed her through the door. I have never seen a woman look so utterly astonished. She said, staring at me, "Well, you are a one!" I slammed the door in her face. Instead of going out to get something to eat I wrote all day and made up the bed myself.

—Jean Rhys, *Smile Please: An Unfinished Autobiography*

I'm afflicted with this disease called insomnia. And it has played a great role in my life and music—my adventures, my nocturnal ramblings, my wanderlust. Between two in the morning and dawn something wonderful happens. A sort of chemical change takes over me and I can listen to music better. I enjoy walking outside better. Even cigarettes seem to taste better.

—Peter Wolf

Night, when words fade and things come alive.
When the destructive analysis of day is done,
and all that is truly important becomes
whole and sound again.

—Antoine de Saint-Exupéry

Daylight is an ugly time of day. So many people are awake, and if I go outside, I know what they're all thinking. They are mainly doing *bad things*. . . .

Nighttime is better. It's not just that it's *quieter*, but I can feel *the absence* of daytime bullshit. People have stopped *scurrying*. (I don't mind them *scurrying* when I'm asleep during the day—I'll find out what they were up to when I wake up and watch the six o'clock news.)

—Frank Zappa, *The Real Frank Zappa Book*

Three score and ten years
is such a stingy ration of time, when there is so much time around. Perhaps that's why some of us are insomniacs; night is so precious that it would be pusillanimous to sleep all through it! A "bad night" is not always a bad thing.

—Brian Aldiss, "Reflections of an Ardent Insomniac"

He liked sleeping alone, and best of all staying awake alone, enjoying his insomnia, thinking his own crazy thoughts that Peg could never understand, listening to the all-night programs on the radio, reading a paragraph here and there about the secret of lobster gumbo or Gregory Peck's love life, figuring out what came next in his own life. . . .

He switched to a West Virginia station where a gentleman farmer was describing how he bored holes in his prize beefsteak tomatoes, filled them with vodka, let them age in the icebox, then ate them for breakfast. The Built-in-Snapper. Delicious. Alvine was about to yell out to Peg to fetch him some beefsteak tomatoes, when he remembered she wasn't there, that he was alone with his darling insomnia.

—Dawn Powell, *The Golden Spur*

Good morning—Midnight—
I'm coming Home—
Day—got tired of Me—
How could I—of Him?

Sunshine was a sweet place—
I liked to stay—
But Morn—didn't want me—now—
So—Goodnight—Day!

—Emily Dickinson

Light Sleeper

directed by **Paul Schrader**(1991)

What do you do when you wake up—clean, sober, mateless, and facing forty—to find yourself with a lucrative but dead-end career as a cocaine-delivery man? When he's not roaming Manhattan serving his upscale clientele, John LeTour (Willem Dafoe) spends sleepless hours prowling his sparsely furnished loft. To unburden his mind, he scribbles his feelings in a notebook—then thoughtfully burns each page. Salting the wound of his midlife crisis, a series of drug-related murders begins to rattle his circle of clients and business partners. Eventually, he must make a choice that will change his life forever—and reveal who his true friends and enemies are.

The Thief Who Couldn't Sleep

by Lawrence Block

There was nothing much to do in that cell. I don't sleep, have not slept in sixteen years—more of that later—so I had the special joy of being bored, not sixteen hours a day, like the normal prisoner, but a full twenty-four.

Evan Michael Tanner hasn't slept a wink since the Korean War, when he took a piece of shrapnel in the sleep center of his brain.

Instead of yearning for repose, Tanner exploits his extra eight hours a day by reading, researching, learning new languages, writing theses for bored graduate students, and playing partisan to a parade of lost causes—Macedonian liberation, restoration of the Stuart pretender to the British throne, Welsh nationalism, Basque separatism, Irish anarchy, and the Armenian plight. Like most hard-boiled detectives, he also has a taste for any ripe and willing woman who happens to cross his path.

Tanner heads for Balakesir when he learns of a cache of gold coins hidden by Armenians fleeing from a Turkish massacre. Along the way he manages to upset the governments of numerous countries on both sides of the Iron Curtain.

According to Block, the story was inspired by an article recounting a few recorded cases of human beings who seem to thrive without any sleep whatsoever. Indeed, his protagonist's missing sleep center does give him a certain edge, as his superior realizes:

"You must have given them the willies. You know their standard interrogation procedure? Nothing fancy, just let a man fall asleep, then wake him up and question him, then let him drift off to sleep again, then more questioning. They hit you at your weakest point that way. But they couldn't do that to you, could they?"

"No."

"Very handy. Never thought of insomnia as a survival mechanism. Very interesting."

"Yes, sir."

the chronometer within

within

Rock Around the Clock—at Your Own Peril

> The harassed middle aged are in love with sleep in the same way as the young are in love with love; chastity is the torment of youth, insomnia of age, and at neither stage of life does it ever seem possible to get enough of what you want.
>
> —A. Alvarez, *Night*

Somewhere inside you, a timepiece is ticking. Circadian rhythms—the biological clocks that rule our routines of waking and sleeping—have an inexorable grip on how we feel and function at every moment.

Circadian means "about, or around, the day," and every animal from the fruit fly to the baboon employs biochemical mechanisms to march to the same twenty-four-hour beat, all adapted to the rotating Earth's cycle of darkness and daylight. For more than three decades, biology textbooks have told us that humans are different, running instead on a twenty-five-hour cycle. But recent research at Harvard University refutes that dogma. "Regardless of other differences between us, our clocks are extremely similar and our timing is first rate," writes Dr. Robert Y. Moore.

What truly separates humans from animals is our ability to expose ourselves to electric light, TVs, and alarm clocks at the flick of a switch—but trouble brews when the trappings of technology seriously upset our internal Timex. Hopping a plane from New York to Athens, for instance, can so disrupt your cycle that you may find yourself walking zombielike through morning traffic or craving souvlaki at four A.M. Switch to the graveyard shift, and it's a good bet you'll be nodding off over your conveyor belt. The disruptions of jet lag and night-shift work can, depending on your constitution, leave you out of phase, out of sorts, and in a rut for days.

Even if you're not a frequent flier or long-haul trucker with white-line fever, the circadian cycle can put a crimp in your life. Sensitive souls sometimes react adversely to changes as innocuous as daylight savings time: On the first work day after the clock "springs ahead," there are more car accidents than any other Monday of the year.

My schedule sort of twirls around the clock. I can't stay on night all the time because every night I work an extra hour or so, editing or recording—pushing it a little later each night—but then, once I go to sleep . . . my "day" keeps changing around. Every three or four weeks I'm back on daylight—and I dread it, because I can't get anything done. The phone rings all the time. All those questions. I can't edit—I can't write—I can't do anything because of the constant interruptions.

—Frank Zappa, *The Real Frank Zappa Book*

Hail to the Chief

World leadership has its privileges, one of them being a rather novel cure for jet lag. When President Lyndon Johnson boarded Air Force One to confer with other heads of state, he insisted on maintaining Washington time at his destination, even if it was halfway around the world. While in Vietnam, he would wake, eat meals, hold meetings, and sleep at his customary times, forcing Vietnamese leaders to adapt to his schedule. Alas, few of us can presume that the world will revolve around us, and must deal with time-zone changes using more conventional methods.

Don't Even *Think* of Sleeping Here

Researchers have identified two times of day—nine to eleven A.M. and seven to nine P.M.—when the mind is so jazzed that even severely sleep-deprived people can't doze off. It's during these so-called forbidden sleep zones that even numbed contestants in dance marathons might notice a second wind coming on.

Conversely, we've all borne the brunt of the midday drowse. From one to four P.M., our brains and bodies become unavoidably sluggish. Urban folklore tells us this is the likely result of a too-heavy lunch, but science informs us that it is in reality the decree of our circadian mistress. Twelve hours later, from one to four A.M., we experience a similar low point—the time when, if weakened by age or disease, we are most likely to die.

Rebels Without a Pause

Studies show that American high schools, malls, and convenience stores are awash with some of the sleepiest teenagers in human history. With the competition for grades (and college admissions) getting more intense every year, and opportunities for extracurricular activities multiplying, today's teens average ninety minutes less shut-eye than the adolescents of a century ago, when even Jules Verne couldn't imagine the implications of surfing the Net.

The transformation of energetic, bright-eyed children into morose, mopey—and hard-to-awaken—teenagers has always given parents a few sleepless nights. But is the change to be blamed on psychology, society, technology, biology, or all four? At Brown University in Providence, Rhode Island, Mary Carskadon is seeking some answers in a chinchillalike rodent from South America called the degu. Because the degu is, like humans, diurnal and slow to mature, Carskadon can examine its adolescent sleep rhythms closely and draw some connections to human behavior—without invading the sanctity of the teen bedroom.

Carskadon's data suggest that, indeed, the onset of puberty coincides with a new phase in our ever-changing circadian rhythms, a passage to the less-wired and more-tired cycles of adulthood, complete with midday energy troughs. Other studies show that in late puberty the body secretes the sleep hormone melatonin at a different time than usual, further disrupting the circadian cycle and making it difficult to fall asleep much before midnight. So today's youth are probably being dealt a multiple whammy: greater societal pressure to achieve, changing internal clocks and hormone levels, and activities that beckon twenty-four–seven.

Acknowledging the obvious, a California congresswoman recently proposed legislation that would have high schools start classes later in the morning, in synch with the changing biological clocks of teens. This "Zs to As" bill was supported by several sleep researchers.

Most of the people I like, or love, or can barely stand are between the ages of forty-five and sixty-five, give or take a year or two at either end, and only about three of them are capable any longer of achieving what was once casually called, and is now wistfully called, a good night's rest.

—James Thurber, "The Watchers of the Night"

Older, Wiser, and Wide Awake

While folk wisdom and anecdotal evidence tell us that we need fewer hours of sleep as we age, modern science is divided on the subject. There is general agreement that, past the age of fifty, sleep becomes lighter and less refreshing, due to a decrease in delta sleep, the deepest phase of slumber. Older folks also fall victim to a conspiracy of factors that derail regular sleep: more aches and pains, more anxieties and depressions, more pills to take (with their sleep-reducing side effects), and, in turn, more sleep medications being prescribed. It is estimated that five million seniors in the United States have severe sleep problems, and half of those folks rely on sleeping pills.

To further complicate matters, recent studies suggest that, as we age, we may become more sensitive to signals from the body's circadian clock. So we're naturally prone to nod off earlier in the evening and wake up earlier in the morning—which may mimic insomnia, for someone accustomed to sleeping past sunrise.

What is insomnia?

The question is rhetorical. I know the answer only too well.

It is to count off and dread in the small hours the fateful harsh strokes of the chime. It is attempting with ineffectual magic to breathe smoothly. It is the burden of a body that abruptly shifts sides. It is shutting the eyelids down tight. It is a state like fever and is assuredly not watchfulness. It is saying over bits of paragraphs read years and years before. It is knowing how guilty you are to be lying awake when others are asleep. It is trying to sink into slumber and being unable to sink into slumber. It is the horror of being and going on being. It is the dubious daybreak.

What is longevity? It is the horror of existing in a human body whose faculties are in decline. It is insomnia measured by decades and not by metal hands. It is carrying the weight of seas and pyramids, of ancient libraries and dynasties, of the dawns that Adam saw. It is being well aware that I am bound to my flesh, to a voice I detest, to my name, to routinely remembering, to Castilian, over which I have no control, to feeling nostalgic for the Latin I do not know. It is trying to sink into death and being unable to sink into death. It is being and continuing to be.

—Jorge Luis Borges, "Two Forms of Insomnia"

Birds Do It. Bees Do It.

Most experts hold that the need for sleep occurs only in higher animals—we warm-blooded creatures blessed with forebrains—but periods of sleeplike inactivity are found among fauna as lowly as cockroaches, bees, grasshoppers, wasps, and moths. Dreamy REM sleep is experienced by most mammals (the spiny anteater and the duck-billed platypus excepted), and even a few birds and reptiles.

Some birds sleep while flying, some fish while swimming. Mice get a solid thirteen hours of sleep, cows a mere three, usually standing. The sloth suspends itself in slumber for up to twenty hours, rivaling only the bat. Your Irish setter will snooze at your feet at the drop of a hat; your cat curls up hundreds of times a day. Chimpanzees, our closest biological cousins, average ten or more hours each day while maintaining sophisticated societies that exhibit an enviable ratio of work to play. And Antarctic researchers, removed from the buzz of civilization, often revert to a ten-hour sleep regimen—suggesting that many modern folks deprive themselves of at least two hours a day.

Evolution dictates that each species develops a sleep cycle best adapted to its survival. Only *homo sapiens* has the bravado to tamper with Mother Nature.

"K" Is for Killer

by Sue Grafton

In the hazy zone where wakefulness fades into sleep, in that leaden moment just before the mind sinks below consciousness, I can sometimes hear [the victims] murmuring. They mourn themselves. They sing a lullaby of the murdered. They whisper the names of their attackers, those men and women who still walk the earth, unidentified, unaccused, unpunished, unrepentant. On such nights, I do not sleep well. I lie awake listening, hoping to catch a syllable, a phrase, straining to discern in that roll call of conspirators the name of one killer.

Kinsey Millhone is the tough-talking private investigator who with every case works her way one letter further along through the alphabet. Here, in the K installment, when grieving mother Janice Kepler asks her to investigate the suspicious death of her daughter Lorna—a part-time secretary with an estate worth around half a million dollars—Millhone uncovers a past that includes prostitution, pornography, and political back-stabbing. Wandering through this shadow land of pain and grief, she finds herself increasingly sleep-deprived the deeper she gets into the case: "It was like hunger—once the peak moment passed, the appetite diminished. . . . Having stayed awake this long, I was confined to further wakefulness."

Eventually, as Millhone goes to bed later and later, her days and nights change places, creating a state that mingles heightened awareness and extreme exhaustion:

I woke up at 5:00 P.M. The eight hours should have been adequate, but as starved as I was for sleep, I felt I was dragging myself out of quicksand. I was still struggling to adjust to the inverted pattern my life had taken. In bed at dawn, up again in the afternoon. I was eating breakfast at lunchtime, dinner in the dead of night, though often that meal turned out to be cold cereal or scrambled eggs and toast, which meant I ate breakfast twice. I was vaguely aware of a psychological shift, a change in my perception now that I'd substituted night for day. Like a form of jet lag, my internal clock was no longer synchronized with the rest of the world's. My usual sense of myself was breaking down, and I wondered if a hidden personality might suddenly emerge as if wakened from a long sleep. My day life was calling, and I was curiously reluctant to answer.

the world between

You're Naked, You're Late, and You Can't Find That Door

Dreaming permits each and every one of us to be quietly and safely insane every night of our lives.

—Charles Fisher, psychiatrist and sleep researcher

In a hyperactive society that has time only for easy labels—young or old, good or bad, rich or poor—have we sacrificed some precious third state of consciousness that might exist between sleeping and waking? And, in turn, sacrificed access to a rich dream world of myths and magic?

This intriguing question is raised by the research of Thomas Wehr, chief of the Clinical Psychology Branch of the National Institutes of Mental Health. Wehr recruited volunteers to recreate the sleep patterns of prehistoric man, whose hours of rest were ruled by the rising and setting of the sun and changes in the seasons.

Over time, volunteers displayed profound changes in their sleep habits, as well as in their waking psychology. They lay down when darkness fell, rested quietly for two hours, then abruptly descended into deep sleep. Four hours later, they awoke from dreamy REM sleep into another two-hour period of waking, quiet rest, followed by a second four-hour stint of heavy slumber. Interestingly, waking in the darkness did not bring the trauma experienced by most insomniacs; the time was pleasurable and meditative. What's more, the volunteers reported—and psychological tests confirmed—that these new rhythms left them feeling more awake, more alive, and more fully aware than they had ever felt before. Wehr speculates that, as modern man gradually phased out this stage between dream life and waking life, he may have lost touch with a primal "wellspring of myths and fantasies."

Interestingly, this reversion to "bimodal" sleep mimics the behavior of most mammals, and this poses an interesting question: Does waking in the middle of the night deserve to be categorized as a "disorder"? Or is insomnia just a symptom of a society that has relegated sleep to an eight-hour stint, transforming a natural time of quiet rest—a period for musing and meditation—into a source of anxiety and medical bills?

Dreaming shows you the kind of world you'd build if left to your own devices. —Stephen LaBerge

Dream Weavers

In California, one guru has dedicated his life to helping you make the most of your dreams. At the Lucidity Institute in Palo Alto, psychophysiologist Stephen LaBerge teaches people how to use their dream lives to influence their waking lives, and vice versa.

LaBerge theorizes that dreaming is a skill that can be learned—and mastered—with diligent practice. In short, he claims that lucid dreamers are able to "program" the content of their dreams, then allow the subconscious to embellish and illuminate that content—with a tangible reality that equals or excels waking life.

The possibilities for dream work and play are infinite: you can live out a fantasy, embark on an adventure, or "sleep on" a creative problem and awake with an insightful solution.

It sounds, and sometimes seems, like New Age hocus-pocus. (One technique involves wearing the "Nova Dreamer," a sleep mask that senses your REM twitches and responds by flashing tiny lights in your eyes, which then appear in your reveries as lightning bolts or suchlike, to make you aware, in middream, that you are indeed dreaming.) Yet lucid dreaming has a long and intriguing history. In 1867, for example, the Marquis Marie Jean Hervey de Saint-Denys, a distinguished French orientalist, published a book called *Dreams and How to Guide Them*, in which he described his deliberate methods for controlling the course of his dreams and creating interactions between dreaming and waking life—a skill he cultivated with the same rigor, he said, as a gymnast training for the trapeze or trampoline.

Several so-called primitive cultures have engaged in similar endeavors. The Senoi people of Malaysia, for instance, were trained from childhood to take control of their dream lives. Under the guidance of tribal leaders, each night's dreams were discussed by the community, and new dreams were induced. The object was to rid individuals of phobias, resolve conflicts within the tribe, and diminish fear of rivals. The sense of confidence and security instilled by these dreams was legendary. To potential enemies, the Senoi seemed magically potent and untouchable. They lived in peace with their neighbors and among themselves.

In the modern world, visitors to Stephen LaBerge's Lucidity Institute have successfully used his techniques to defeat shyness, defuse nightmares, surmount writer's block, and overcome grief by resolving relationships with dead loved ones, as well as make mad love to a Victoria's Secret supermodel without ever making her acquaintance.

John-A-Dreams

Dreams are imperfections of sleep; even so is consciousness the imperfection of waking.

Dreams are impurities in the circulation of the blood;

even so is consciousness a disorder of life.

Dreams are without proportion, without good

sense, without truth; so also is consciousness.

Awake from dream, the truth is known: awake

from waking, the Truth is The Unknown.

— Aleister Crowley, *The Book of Lies*

He walked toward the sheets of flame. They did not bite his flesh, they caressed him and flooded him without heat or combustion. With relief, with humiliation, with terror, he understood that he also was an illusion, that someone else was dreaming him. —Jorge Luis Borges, "The Circular Ruins" Sleep is an under-ocean dipped into each night/At morning, awake dripping, gasping, eyes stinging. —Jim Morrison, *The Lords* Emerged from sleep the dream fades. It is a deep sea plant which dies out of water. It dies on my sheets. Its reign mystifies me. I admire its fables. I take advantage of it to live a double life. I never make use of it. —Jean Cocteau, "On Dreams"

the waking dream

In the British romantic poet Samuel Taylor Coleridge's preface to his dreamy reverie "Kubla Khan" (subtitled "Or, A Vision in a Dream. A Fragment"), he sets forth the legend of its composition.

On the night he wrote the piece, he says, he had taken a narcotic and fallen asleep while reading this sentence from a book entitled *Purchas's Pilgrimage*: "Here the Khan Kubla commanded a palace to be built, and a stately garden thereunto. And thus ten miles of fertile ground were inclosed with a wall."

In Coleridge's opiated sleep, that passage induced a fantastic dream, from which he awoke to scribble down three hours later—more a feverish transcriber, he claims, than a poet. After an hour's interruption, by then retaining only a dim recollection of the vision, he was unable to complete the poem, in the way that a dream becomes wispier as the day progresses, despite all attempts to return to its technicolor embrace.

Pointing to the unfinished poem's obvious order, rhythm, and structure, critics question Coleridge's apologia that the poem is really a dream effortlessly recalled. Even so, the realm it describes is surely one of the most exotic, lulling, and magical places ever imagined in a dream or otherwise:

In Xanadu, did Kubla Khan
A stately pleasure dome decree:
Where Alph, the sacred river, ran
Through caverns measureless to man
    Down to a sunless sea.
So twice five miles of fertile ground
With walls and towers were girdled round:
And there were gardens bright with sinuous rills,
Where blossomed many an incense-bearing tree;
And here were forests ancient as the hills,
Enfolding sunny spots of greenery....

...I have had a most rare
vision. I have had a dream, past the wit of man to
say what dream it was: man is but an ass, if he go
about to expound this dream. Methought I was—there
is no man can tell what. Methought I was,—and
methought I had,—but man is but a patched fool, if
he will offer to say what methought I had.

—Bottom in Shakespeare's *A Midsummer Night's Dream*, waking after a night
of love such as he will never experience again, as a donkey or otherwise

In a Wonderland they be,
Dreaming as the days go by,
Dreaming as the summers die.
Ever drifting down the stream—
Lingering in the golden gleam—
Life, what is it but a dream?

—Lewis Carroll, *Through the Looking Glass*

Sometimes a thousand twangling instruments
Will hum about mine ears, and sometime voices
That, if I then had waked after long sleep,
Will make me sleep again: and then, in dreaming,
The clouds methought would open and show riches
Ready to drop upon me that, when I waked,
I cried to dream again.

—Caliban in Shakespeare's *The Tempest*

Our Daily Dose of Madness
Roaming the streets of nighttime London, his powers of empathy undiminished by lack of sleep, Charles Dickens found himself one night outside Bethlehem Hospital—a typical Victorian insane asylum more commonly known as Bedlam:

Are not the sane and the insane equal at night as the sane lie a-dreaming? Are not all of us outside this hospital, who dream, more or less in the condition of those inside it, every night of our lives? Are we not nightly persuaded, as they daily are, that we associate preposterously with kings and queens, emperors and empresses, and notabilities of all sorts? Do we not nightly jumble events and personages and times and places, as these do daily? Are we not sometimes troubled by our own sleeping inconsistencies; and do we not vexedly try to account for them or excuse them, just as these do sometimes in respect of their waking delusions? Said an afflicted man to me, when I was last in a hospital like this, "Sir, I can frequently fly." I was half ashamed to reflect that so could I—by night. Said a woman to me on the same occasion, "Queen Victoria frequently comes to dine with me, and her Majesty and I dine off peaches and macaroni in our night-gowns and his Royal Highness the Prince Consort does us the honour to make a third on horseback in a Field-Marshal's uniform." Could I refrain from reddening with consciousness when I remembered the amazing royal parties I myself had given (at night), the unaccountable viands I had put on table, and my extraordinary manner of conducting myself on those distinguished occasions? I wonder that the great master who knew everything, when he called Sleep the death of each day's life, did not call Dreams the insanity of each day's sanity.

—Charles Dickens, "Night Walks"

No amount of skepticism and criticism has yet enabled me to regard dreams as negligible occurrences. Often enough they appear senseless, but it is obviously we who lack the sense and ingenuity to read the enigmatic message from the nocturnal realm of the psyche.

—Carl Jung, "Dreams"

People who insist on telling their dreams are among the terrors of the breakfast table.

—Max Beerbohm

The Insomniac's
Film Festival

A Nightmare on Elm Street

directed by **Wes Craven** (1984)

Nancy, a fresh-faced adolescent, is wrenched awake from a nightmare: She's been fleeing from a murderous fiend with a scarred face, a striped shirt, and gloves adorned with razor-sharp knives. When she learns that friends have seen the same ghoul in their dreams, the teen population of placid Elm Street shares a communal shiver. When one of them dies in her sleep—in a particularly grisly fashion—the survivors realize that this is no run-of-the-mill bogeyman. Terrified of sleep, they begin an ordeal of enforced insomnia, fighting fatigue while they work to uncover the dream killer's supernatural secrets—and how to stop him.

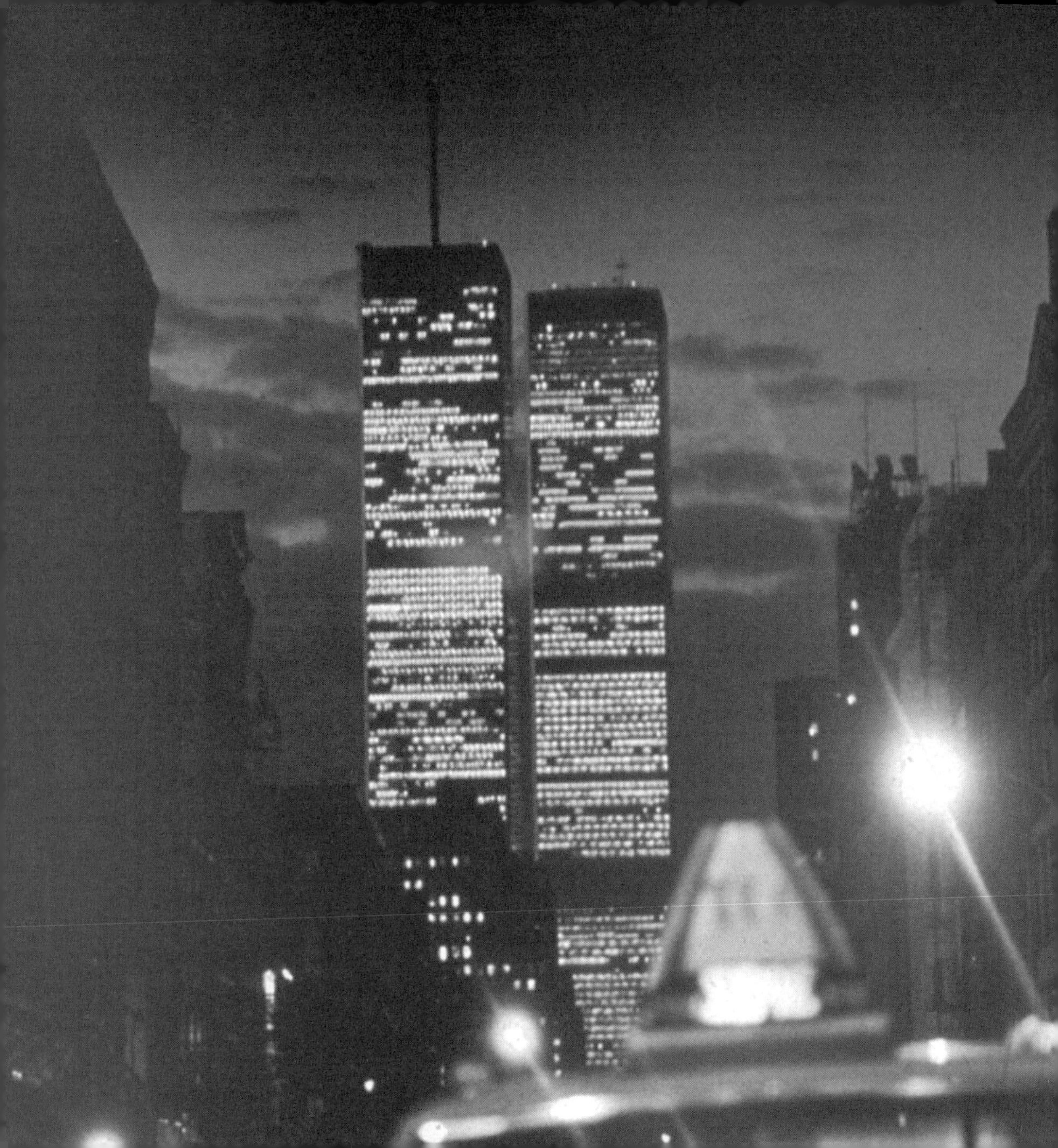

the
city
that never
sleeps

The Bronx Is Up and the Battery's Down

Do city dwellers toss and turn more than their country counterparts? Hard to say. But based on anecdotal evidence, New York City—never lacking for nocturnal amusements or annoyances—must reign as the nerve center of insomnia.

Not only are there more things to do there at three A.M. than anywhere else, there are more things to fret about: the nightly terrors come at you with the relentlessness of automatically pitched baseballs. (Fall asleep, and one might hit you so hard you never wake up.) What with the city's endemic loneliness, out-of-control cabbies, complex social order, high rents, and steady influx of overachievers, it's a wonder *anybody* gets any shut-eye in this town.

In the middle of the night sometimes, above the skyscrapers, across hundreds of high walls, the cry of a tugboat would meet my insomnia, reminding me that this desert of iron and cement was also an island.

—Albert Camus, "The Rains of New York"

How pleasant the rooms were, how comforting the distresses of New Yorkers, their insomnias filled with words, their patient exegesis of surprising terrors. Divorce, abandonment, the unacceptable and the unattainable, ennui filled with action, sad, tumultuous middle-age years shaken by crashings, uprootings, coups, desperate renewals. Weaknesses discovered, hidden forces unmasked, predictions, what will last and what is doomed, what will start and what will end. Work and love; the idle imagining the pleasure of the working ones. Those who work and their quizzical frowns, which ask: When will something new come to me? After all I am a sort of success.

—Elizabeth Hardwick, *Sleepless Nights*

I can still hear the sounds of those Methodist bells,
I'd taken the cure and had just gotten through,
Stayin' up for days in the Chelsea Hotel
Writin' "Sad-Eyed Lady of the Lowlands" for you.
—Bob Dylan, "Sara"

New York makes a noise like no other city I know. . . . Wherever you are in

New York City what you hear is a steady roar, like a turbine at full throttle,

churning out energy and power. The first time I noticed it I thought it was

the air-conditioning, yet when I switched off the unit and opened a window

the noise became louder. It has nothing to do with car horns; they are mere-

ly treble flourishes over its moving bass. It's not the wind either, although the

wind, booming around the skyscrapers, is part of it. The New York noise is a

steady state, an environment. It is deep and constant, like the sea, and the car

horns, sirens and steam-brakes are the spume on its surface. . . .

Night life, too, is a democratic right, freely available to everyone,

regardless of race, colour or creed. New Yorkers have always taken pride

in the brilliance and liveliness of their city after dark. Jimmy Walker, who

was Mayor of New York in the 1920s, said it was a sin to go to bed the

same day you got up, and "the great white way" is a permanent celebra-

tion, a triumph over the natural adversity of darkness.

—A. Alvarez, *Night*

You are not the kind of guy who would be at a place like this at this time of the morning. But here you are, and you cannot say that the terrain is entirely unfamiliar, although the details are fuzzy. You are at a nightclub talking to a girl with a shaved head. The club is either Heartbreak or the Lizard Lounge. . . . The night has already turned on that imperceptible pivot where two A.M. changes to six A.M. You know this moment has come and gone, but you are not yet willing to concede that you have crossed the line beyond which all is gratuitous damage and the palsy of unraveled nerve endings. Somewhere back there you could have cut your losses, but you rode past that moment on a comet trail of white powder and now you are trying to hang on to the rush. . . .

It is even worse than you expected, stepping out into the morning. The glare is like a mother's reproach. The sidewalk sparkles cruelly. Visibility unlimited. The downtown warehouses look serene and restful in this beveled light. An uptown cab passes and you start to wave, then realize you have no money. The cab stops.

You jog over and lean in the window. "I guess I'll walk after all."

"Asshole." He leaves rubber.

You start north, holding a hand over your eyes. Trucks rumble up Hudson Street, bearing provisions into the sleeping city. You turn east. On Seventh Avenue an old woman with a hive of rollers on her head walks a German shepherd. The dog is rooting in the cracks of the sidewalk, but as you approach he stiffens into a pose of terrible alertness. The woman looks at you as if you were something that had just crawled out of the ocean trailing ooze and slime. An eager, tentative growl ripples the shepherd's throat. "Good Pooky," she says. The dog makes a move but she chokes it back. You give them a wide berth.

—Jay McInerney, *Bright Lights, Big City*

> Big party in Harlem, at Allen [Ginsberg]'s and Russell Durgin's. I spent another three days without eating or sleeping to speak of, just drinking and squinting and sweating....
>
> —Jack Kerouac, journal entry, July 3, 1948

Like a nun who renounces worldly life, I became enslaved to rigid routines: not travelling because crossing time zones and sleeping in strange beds almost guaranteed sleepless nights.

Then I moved to New York City, a place where somebody's always up and nothing's ever truly still. I discovered twenty-four hour CNN, talked to stockbroker friends who woke up at 3:00 A.M. to check the Tokyo market and watched midnight fax transmissions from Europe unfurl on the floor of my one-room apartment/office.

—Lois Nesbitt, *Mirabella* magazine

Rain again this morning. A bad night, and finally gave up much too early—tired, miserable, tense—to hear the truck traffic off Fifty-eighth Street heading for Queensboro Bridge. But am coming back to myself as I write this after coffee. Am listening to the first Chopin concerto (Arthur Rubinstein), and feel better. The cars skid and whistle in the rain. Glistening drops of champagne fall off the imaginary piano to my left. Now Frederic is playful: the quick last movement. Rumble, skid, and whistle from the traffic in the rain. The tires go round and round and round. My heart leaps over the abyss of the night, reaching as on a merry-go-round for the ring that welcomes on the other side.

—Alfred Kazin, *A Lifetime Burning in Every Moment*

During the day he walked around, wrapped up in himself, figuring out his music, watching TV or composing when he felt like it. Sometimes he paced for four or five days in a row, walking the streets at first, going south as far as Sixtieth, north as far as Seventieth, west as far as the river and three blocks east, then gradually restricting his orbit until he was walking around the block and then sticking to the rooms of the apartment, pacing non-stop, hugging the walls, never touching the piano, never sitting—then sleeping for two days straight through.

— Geoff Dyer on the insomnia of jazz pianist Thelonious Monk, in *But Beautiful: A Book About Jazz*

You'll never sleep tonight.
Trains will betray you, cars confess
Their destinations,

Whether you like it
Or not.

They want more
Than to be in
Your dreams.

They want to tell you
A story.

They yammer all night and then
The birds take over,
Jeering as only
The well-rested can.

—Cornelius Eady, "Insomnia"

The Insomniac's
Film Festival

Taxi Driver

directed by

Martin Scorsese (1976)

Travis Bickle (Robert DeNiro) can't sleep—so the troubled Vietnam vet takes a job as a night-shift cab driver in the grimy streets of 1970s New York. The people he meets in his midnight prowls—anonymous fares, a teenage streetwalker and her pimp, a girl-next-door politico, fellow night-crawling cabbies at a twenty-four-hour diner—become characters in a waking nightmare, colored by Bickle's own obsessions and delusions. Alone in his stark one-room apartment, he talks to his reflection in the mirror, plotting revenge against a society that casts him as a loser and a loner. Ultimately, his rage explodes in a bout of murderous violence—and a strange fate that offers a shred of hope.

forever
wakeful?

True Stories and Tall Tales

The doctors told me, "You're

—Keith Ward, a Californian who suffers from jactacio capitis nocturna (nighttime head-bangi

Folklore is peppered with tales of individuals who, through some mutation or injury, seem to exist on no sleep at all. While science is divided as to whether these hard-to-find people are clever charlatans or genuine flukes of nature, the stories keep coming. One journalist journeyed to Cuba in 1986 for the tale of Tomas Izquierdo, a man who never sleeps:

The only outward sign that Tomas Izquierdo has lived without normal sleep for 40 years is the pair of dark glasses protecting his sensitive eyes.

The former textile worker is a mentally alert and young-looking 53, and he and his second wife recently had a son. Yet a large dossier of medical evidence suggests that he lost his ability to sleep at the end of World War II and has remained awake ever since.

"As far as we know, no case like it has been reported in medical literature anywhere in the world," says Dr. Pedro Garcia Fleites, one of Cuba's leading psychiatrists, who has treated Izquierdo for the past 16 years.

In 1970, Garcia Fleites and a team of doctors at Havana Psychiatric Hospital kept Izquierdo under constant observation for nearly two weeks. Even when he rested with his eyes closed, the electroencephalograms continued to register the brain activity of a person fully awake.

"He has no natural sleep. The nearest thing Tomas gets to sleep is a drowsiness produced by drugs prescribed for him," the psychiatrist said in an interview.

Like the rest of us who cannot survive more than a few days without sleep, Izquierdo suffers from exhaustion and needs periodic rest.

Even in a state of drug-induced narcosis, however, he is unable to escape completely from the consciousness that has haunted him since 1945.

"I dream just as I would say everybody else dreams. The difference is that I know positively that I am awake and that I am active," Izquierdo said at his home in this small town near Havana.

He and Garcia Fleites have different ideas about the origin of his insomnia. According to the psychiatrist and other doctors familiar with the case, Izquierdo's sleep mechanism was prob-

ably damaged by an attack of encephalitis—an inflammation of the inner brain—when he was 13.

Izquierdo thinks his insomnia derives from a psychological trauma he suffered during an operation to remove his tonsils. A throat hemorrhage sent blood spurting out of his mouth and the terrified adolescent thought he was dying.

The horrific sensation of dying subsequently repeated itself in nightmares, and Izquierdo says that he began resisting sleep to avoid them. According to his own account, within a few weeks he found he had stopped sleeping altogether.

Since then, more than 40 doctors have tried hypnosis, electroshock treatment, acupuncture and experimental drugs to restore Izquierdo's ability to sleep.

Izquierdo has even resorted to spiritual mediums and voodoo doctors, but all have apparently failed to allow him to sleep.

Affectionately known in San Antonio de Los Baños as "Tomas who doesn't sleep," Izquierdo used to work double shifts at the local textile factory. He was retired in 1968 on medical grounds when symptoms connected with his inability to sleep became evident.

According to Garcia Fleites, Izquierdo's memory began to fail, and he showed a progressive lack of self-confidence.

Izquierdo himself admits that he now finds it difficult to remember dates or retain the contents of a book.

At present, he passes the time doing odd jobs for friends and neighbors and driving couples to weddings in his immaculately kept 1955 Chevrolet Bel Air.

Transcendental meditation has become his most effective form of relaxation, and on most nights he rests for a few hours from 3 or 4 A.M. onward, meditating or drifting into a drug-induced stupor. Sometimes Izquierdo feels that he can still go happily for several days without rest.

"But some days it is just the opposite," he says. "There are days when I am good for nothing. I feel drained, drained, drained, mainly in a mental sense, but physically as well.

"It's a tragedy," Izquierdo says, "a tragedy within my own self."

—Robert Powell, Reuters News Service

Edison's Lamentable Legacy

We are always hearing people talk about "loss of sleep" as a calamity. They better call it loss of time, vitality, and opportunities.

—Thomas Edison

There is no small irony in the fact that Thomas Alva Edison, the inventor of the incandescent light bulb and countless electric amusements, may also go down in history as the father of modern sleeplessness.

Before electricity became practical, cheap, and widely used, humankind set their internal clocks by the sun. After Edison, all hell broke loose. Factories could run around the clock. Recorded music and films expanded options for leisure activity. And the night, once a lulling downtime illuminated only by the moon and stars, became a garish new venue for waking pursuits.

By the end of the nineteenth century, most people were sleeping, on average, two hours less per night than a century earlier. This was quite pleasing to Mr. Edison, who viewed sleep as an obstacle to man's true calling—work. "Anything which tends to slow work down is a waste," he claimed.

Edison's work ethic was so strong that, when overcome with fatigue in the midst of a project, he would nap in his chair with a brass ball in each hand. As he drifted off to sleep, his grip would loosen and the balls would fall, waking him for the next spasm of diligent innovation.

During a rare vacation from his laboratories, Edison smiled upon his handiwork: "When I went through Switzerland in a motor-car . . . I noted the effect of artificial light on the inhabitants. Where . . . electric light had been developed, everyone seemed normally intelligent. Where these appliances did not exist, and the natives went to bed with the chickens, staying there till daylight, they were far less intelligent."

Edison's equation of wakefulness with smarts—and sleep with sloth—has dogged the modern world ever since.

Receiving dept., 3 A.M.
staff cuts have socked up the overage
directives are posted.
no callbacks, complaints.
everywhere is calm.

Hong Kong is present
Taipei awakes
all talk of circadian rhythm

I see today with a newsprint fray
my night is colored headache grey
daysleeper

the bull and the bear are marking
their territories
they're leading in the blind with
their international glories

I'm the screen, the blinding light
I'm the screen, I work at night.

I see today with a newsprint fray
my night is colored headache grey
don't wake me with so much.
daysleeper.

I cried the other night
I can't even say why
fluorescent flat caffeine lights
its furious balancing

I'm the screen, the blinding light
I'm the screen, I work at night
I see today . . .
don't wake me with so much. the
ocean machine is set to 9
I'll squeeze into heaven and valentine
my bed is pulling me
gravity
daysleeper. daysleeper.
daysleeper. daysleeper. daysleeper.
—REM, "Daysleeper"

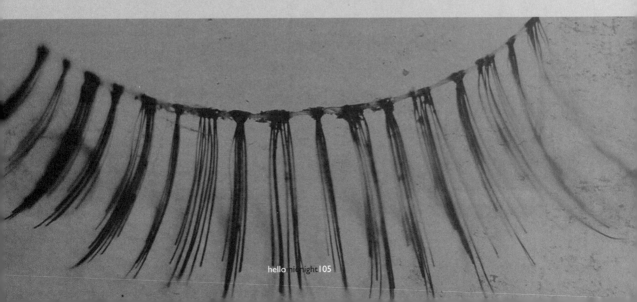

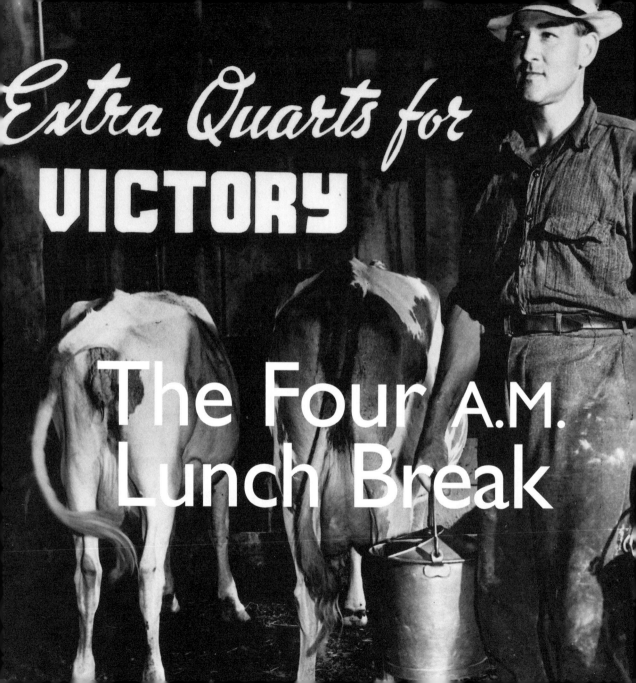

> Those who work at night are one body, and sometimes they are aware of their larger self. There are watchmen, helmsmen, surgeons, purveyors, thieves, bakers, mothers, beginners, and all the others. Together they are alive under the presence of the spaces of night, and it seems as though their veins might go on growing out of them into the dark sky, like a tree.
>
> —W. S. Merwin, "At Night"

The tale of Eli Whitney's invention of the cotton gin—and its morphing of the socioeconomics of the American South—is told in every high school history textbook. Another of Whitney's brainchildren, however, warped the history of American sleep: faced with the challenge of quickly producing ten thousand muskets for President Thomas Jefferson's federal army, Whitney's answer was the machine tool—a mechanism for the precise manufacture of interchangeable parts.

Whitney's innovation was only a first step. Add to it the light bulb and the conveyor belt—which Henry Ford did to create the modern factory assembly line—and you've completed the recipe for the American system of mass production. Man, the tool-making animal, had finally crafted a tool that was his master, a tool that dictated its own frenetic pace. The relentlessness of automated production—and its corollary, the relentless pressure to consume—soon became the twin engines that drove the twentieth century.

Today, more than 26 million Americans (more than a quarter of men and 17 percent of women) are shift workers. Many of them regularly float between day and night shifts—an ideal way, say sleep researchers, to destroy one's natural sleep and wakefulness rhythms. One study found that people with ever-shifting schedules—doctors, nurses, pilots, truckers, police, firefighters—are five times more likely to have mental-health problems than those who work days only. Such workers, while well served by twenty-four-hour doughnut shops and six A.M. bar openings, are ill served by living out of whack with both nature and the dominant mode of society.

The Light in the Kremlin Window

History is riddled with tales of leaders whose boldness was measured, in part, by their defiance of sleep.

Napoleon's conquest of Europe was said to be fueled by his superhuman vigor; the story goes that he could spend a half hour atop a hill, meditating on horseback, then return refreshed and ready for battle. Winston Churchill reportedly slept only a few hours a night. American presidents from Kennedy to Clinton are celebrated for their "boundless energy" and 'round-the-clock workdays. Joseph Stalin often wheedled the Soviet masses to put in longer hours, proffering himself as an example: "Look up at my office in the Kremlin. Even in the middle of the night you will see the lights on because I am at my desk working for Russia."

Undoubtedly, leadership extracts extraordinary demands. But the truth is, great leaders have always been great spin doctors. Historians cite eyewitness accounts of Napoleon's fatigue and poor performance at critical meetings and battles, including Waterloo; Churchill himself admitted, "When the war started, I had to sleep during the day because that was the only way I could cope with my responsibilities." Kennedy's intimates report that he often indulged in, and may have been addicted to, amphetamines. And despite the fact that Stalin's office lights burned into the wee hours, the brazen mythmaker often slipped out the back door and went home for a good night's rest.

Sleep, Sloth, and Genius

Is excessive wakefulness a mark of genius?

Legend has it that Leonardo da Vinci—painter, sculptor, architect, anatomist, inventor, and archetypal Renaissance man—slept only fifteen minutes every four hours. (Of course, his feverish concentration when doing anatomical drawings might be due to viewing corpses in an era before refrigeration.)

On the other hand, Albert Einstein—perhaps the greatest scientific mind of the twentieth century—routinely snoozed for up to eleven hours a night and still managed to profoundly alter our understanding of the universe.

Ultimately, the cliché of the frenzied creative genius is probably a blend of verifiable fact, public relations puffery, and personal mythmaking. As Samuel Johnson, the prolific British writer and compiler of the first English dictionary, once admitted, "I have, all my life long, been lying [in bed] till noon; yet I tell all young men, and tell them with great sincerity, that nobody who does not rise early will ever do any good."

Speeding Without Crashing?

People have been pulling "all-nighters" since some sadistic instructor first invented the concept of the deadline. But the substances used to help fight fatigue have always had a downside, from caffeine's churning stomach to the teeth-grinding jitters that accompany amphetamines and cocaine. But now a new drug called Modafinil offers the promise—and the threat—of days of wakefulness without dependence, withdrawal, or devastating side effects.

Originally developed to keep soldiers battle-ready for long stretches, Modafinil has been used successfully in France to treat narcolepsy, and has recently been approved by the United States Food and Drug Administration. In Canadian military experiments, the drug kept subjects awake and working productively for a full three days. Their performance improved in much the same way it might have had they been given amphetamines, but they simply felt awake, not high, and they returned to normal sleep cycles easily, without "crashing." The drug's only consistent side effect was instilling a sense of overconfidence: subjects felt their proficiency was better than it actually was.

And therein lies the rub: a sleep-deprived worker knows he's taking risks, but a sleep-deprived yet supremely confident worker can be downright dangerous. If workaholics flock to Modafinil, society may find itself dealing with a new—and difficult to detect—breed of "drug problem."

The Beggars Trilogy

by Nancy Kress

"I want to sleep, Daddy."

"No, you don't, sweetheart. Sleep is just lost time, wasted life. It's a little death."

What would it be like if we *never* needed to sleep?

This science fiction trilogy—*Beggars in Spain, Beggars and Choosers,* and *Beggars Ride*—attempts to answer that question, while at the same time exploring myriad ethical quandaries about nanotechnology and the nature of prejudice, fear, and class struggle.

Leisha Camden is one of a new group of people called the Sleepless, who have been genetically modified before birth to require no sleep. Her twin sister Alice is not, and thus a Sleeper. The conflict between the two, and the Sleepers and Sleepless, provides the *leitmotif* running throughout the books: how does society adjust to an elite group of people who have 30 percent more time to study, think, and work? And do the Sleepless, who are also immune to disease and hunger, bear responsibility for the well-being of a sleeping society that they perceive as inferior—as beggars?

As the Sleepless quickly establish dominance in their respective fields, the genetically unaltered respond with envy, wrath, and even violence toward them. Although superior in almost every respect—including outstanding health and longevity—the Sleepless are hampered by their inability to dream and lack of appreciation for art.

When in the third volume the Sleepless cease distributing Change—the miracle substance that prevents disease in all humans—a class war is ignited.

The X-Files, "Sleepless"

directed by

Howard Gordon

"The truth is still out there, but it's never been more dangerous."
Sleeplessness has been a long-running motif on the popular television show *The X-Files*. Protagonist Fox Mulder himself is plagued by chronic insomnia.

The script for the episode "Sleepless," an exploration of the effects of extreme sleep deprivation, began with scriptwriter Howard Gordon's own bout with insomnia. "I wrote a whole other script, and I knew even as I was writing it that this was not right," Gordon recalled. "I was two weeks away from deadline . . . and was basically up for two nights and two days panicking. Out of that came the idea—what if this guy couldn't sleep for twenty-five years?"

The episode opens with a sleep-disorder specialist, Dr. Saul Grissom, dialing 911 as flames threaten to engulf him. He is found burned to death—but his apartment shows no signs of any fire. Soon after, a bleary-eyed ex-Marine, who had been stationed in Southeast Asia with Grissom twenty-four years before, is gunned down by a spectral group of Vietnamese peasants.

Mulder visits Grissom's sleep-disorder clinic and learns of a past project to create the perfect soldier: one who never needs to sleep. The experiment went awry, though, and the military unwittingly let loose a platoon of uncontrollable killing machines. The only surviving member of the test unit is the Bible-spouting Augustus Cole, who's decided that it's time to atone for a particularly brutal massacre that occurred exactly twenty-four years before . . .

why
worry
today
when
you
can

worry tonight?

Eighty-five Topics of Regret, Remorse,
Resentment, and Recrimination

I just get tangled in the sheets

I swim in sweat three inches deep

I just lay back and claim defeat . . .

My hands are locked up tight in fists

My mind is racing, filled with lists

of things to do and things I've done

Another sleepless night's begun.

—Barenaked Ladies, "Who Needs Sleep"

• What if everything my mother told me **turns out to be true?**

• Is there more hair than usual in my comb?

• Will they revoke my degree if they discover that my senior thesis on pedophilia in Shakespeare was stolen from a back issue of the *Journal of the Modern Language Association?*

• **Is every former classmate more successful than I am?**

• Why did I have unprotected sex with my personal trainer?

• Will I become a bag lady?

• Will I ever have children?

• **If I have children, will they become drug addicts?**

• Why didn't I buy a house fifteen years ago, instead of a new Toyota?

• What if I'm audited and I have to justify spending more on meals than I earned all year?

• **Am I an alcoholic?**

• Why did I buy that hideous orange mohair sweater that makes me look like a refugee from the set of *Friends?*

- How much money have I wasted on lattes over the past ten years?
- **If I'd invested my latte money in an IRA, how much would I be worth?**
- Now that it's too late to open an IRA, what will I live on when I'm too old to work?
- Is there life after Prozac?
- Is it too late to learn a foreign language?
- If I color my hair when I'm pregnant, will I poison my child?
- Why was I wearing sweats when I ran into my ex?
- Is it time to start dressing my age?
- **Will I end up looking exactly like my father?**
- Is it too late to embark on the Western canon?
- I should have stuck with the piano lessons.
- How much have I spent on therapy?
- **Is she faking her orgasms?**
- What if my student-loan company tracks me down in Prague?
- Why did I agree to split the winning lottery ticket?
- The Pomeranian seemed cute in the window.
- **If life is a cabaret, who's paying the cover?**
- My inner child gets out more than I do.
- Our son is dating a telemarketer.
- Should I join the Peace Corps or become a paralegal?
- Will the electromagnetic field from my electric blanket give me cancer?
- **How do I tell the other postal workers they didn't get the promotion?**
- Am I eating enough cruciferous vegetables?
- I don't have buns of steel.
- Why did I tell him I adore children?

- Can I use the insomnia defense to get out of jury duty?
- **Does the FBI keep a file on the videos I rent?**
- Does my personal fragrance communicate "quiet desperation"?
- Can I really date a man who sports a beret?
- Is that a lump?
- Why has my daughter adorned her room with Sylvia Plath posters?
- Why did I agree to natural childbirth?
- When did I stop looking for Mr. Goodbar and start eating Snickers?
- If I start reusing empty margarine tubs, am I turning into my mother?
- Why didn't I hold on to my '69 orange Beetle?
- His thighs are smaller than mine.
- Her thighs are larger than mine.
- **Why did I describe myself as "petite, nurturing, and playful" in that personal ad?**
- Why did I tell my hairdresser I wanted to look like Demi Moore?
- Why did I use the word *paradigm* during the job interview?
- I have less than a year to fall in love, get married, and procreate before menopause.
- **Why did I buy a mauve car?**
- They stole my idea for clumping cat litter.
- Is there a single woman over thirty who doesn't live with two cats?
- Is there a single man over thirty who isn't a sociopath?
- Who's reading my e-mail?
- If we miss our deadline, will they cancel our book contract?
- If Ally McBeal can't find a man, how will I?
- Why did I tell her I was a nonsmoker?
- Should I wear a **miniskirt** to traffic court?

- How long before the stock market crashes?

• I'm too young to be a den mother.

• What if our baby looks like Karl Malden?

• Can I be denied a loan application because of overdue library books?

• What if one of my kids pursues a career in advertising?

• Do I really want to work for a company seeking "a high-energy self-starter who thinks out of the box and thrives on deadlines"?

• I need to lose twenty pounds by dawn.

• Is my new computer already obsolete?

• Why did I think I would ever ride a mountain bike?

• Why did I buy a beanbag chair?

• What if my ex-wife testifies?

• What if my yoga instructor sees me at McDonald's?

• What if she finds out I've been calling Mistress Ilsa's Hotline?

• Why did I marry for real estate?

• How much would I be worth if I'd invested $10,000 in eBay stock when I had the chance?

• I should have known when I spotted the humidor in her bedroom.

• Why did I toss out those Beanie Babies?

• Why did I agree to go snowboarding on the first date?

• Did I just answer a blind Help Wanted ad for my current position?

• Now that I'm engaged, what if I meet my soul mate?

• Our baby-sitter likes to read Stephen King.

• Now that I've seen my boss in a towel at the health club, I'll never get the promotion.

• I am likely to have a midlife crisis before I have a life.

• How will I ever get up in the morning?

pseudoinsomnia

Almost as Brutal as the Real Thing

> *He's such a terrible insomniac, he even dreams he's awake.*
>
> —Jewish joke

"I didn't sleep a wink last night."

How often have you heard—or uttered—this complaint? And how true is it?

Back in the early 1970s, it was believed that fully half of those being treated for chronic insomnia were actually "pseudoinsomniacs"—people convinced that they enjoy little or no sleep, despite an absence of verifiable physiological symptoms. Apparently, we are unreliable narrators when it comes to remembering whether we slept for one hour—or eight.

Since diagnostic techniques have become more sophisticated, the number of faux insomniacs being treated has dropped to about 10 percent. According to sleep doctors, people take the news that they are not truly sleep deprived in a variety of ways that range from relief to disbelief to anger—and even threats of malpractice suits.

The few, the proud, the sleepless.

A classic pseudoinsomniac is Marcel Proust's Aunt Leonie, a woman who based her reputation on the fact that she was never able to sleep: **Unfortunately, having formed the habit of thinking aloud, she did not always take care to see that there was no one in the adjoining room, and I would often hear her saying to herself: "I must not forget that I never slept a wink"—for "never sleeping a wink" was her great claim to distinction, and one admitted and respected in our household vocabulary: in the morning Françoise would not "call" her, but would simply "go in" to her; during the day, when my aunt wished to take a nap, we used to say just that she wished to "be quiet" or to "rest"; and when in conversation she so far forgot herself as to say "what woke me up," or "I dreamed that," she would blush and at once correct herself.**

—Marcel Proust, *Remembrance of Things Past*

Breathless

Marilyn Monroe attributed her chronic insomnia (and infatuation with death) to her memory of an attempted suffocation when she was thirteen months old. Interestingly, she didn't start telling this story until the mid-fifties—making it either a recovered memory or an inventive attempt to explain away her erratic behavior on (and off) the set. Film critic Pauline Kael surmised that Monroe may have derived the idea from her role as a psychopathic baby-sitter who attacks a little girl in the 1952 film *Don't Bother to Knock*.

So convincing were these dreams of lying awake that he awoke from them each morning in complete exhaustion and fell right back to sleep. —Joseph Heller

I am sure many times too that I slept without knowing it—but I never slept knowing it. —Ernest Hemingway, "Now I Lay Me"

He sleeps well who knows not that he sleeps ill. —Publicus Cyrus

One day, the man emerged from his sleep as if from a viscous desert, looked at the useless afternoon light which he immediately confused with the dawn, and understood that he had not dreamed. All that night and all day long, the intolerable lucidity of insomnia fell upon him. —Jorge Luis Borges, "The Circular Ruins"

My sleep waking, it deserves

There is no doubt that Velchaninov did sleep and that he fell asleep very soon after the candle was put out; he remembered this clearly afterward. But all the time he was asleep,

is so near hardly the name.

—Raymond Chandler, *The Big Sleep*

up to the very moment that he woke up, he dreamed that he was not asleep, and that in spite of his exhaustion he could not fall asleep. —Fyodor Dostoyevsky

the waking nightmare

Voices, Visions, and Other Distractions

> # Living is a disease from which sleep gives us relief eight hours a day.
>
> —Sebastien Chamfort

After even a few days without sleep, strolling a familiar street can seem as foreign as wandering through a Dalí painting. The symptoms of sleep deprivation mimic those of psychosis: visual and aural hallucinations, elaborate waking fantasies, memory loss, and, eventually, acute paranoia.

Well aware of this, interrogators during the Spanish Inquisition withheld sleep to break the will of prisoners, who would confess or betray trusts while experiencing temporary bouts of madness.

Sleep deprivation has been used for good as well. In 1959, for example, as a stunt to raise money for charity, the New York disc jockey Peter Tripp spent two hundred hours awake in a glass booth in Times Square. He survived the ordeal, but not without signs of mental decay. Toward the end, he could barely stumble his way through the alphabet, and he saw spiders weaving cobwebs on his shoes.

When the time came to do his daily three-hour radio show, though, he always rose to the occasion. Surprisingly, performance of mental tasks doesn't necessarily deteriorate among the sleep-deprived. What does plummet is motivation. Says researcher Wilse Webb of the University of Florida (in *Losing Sleep* by Lydia Dotto), "We don't find that the capacity for things like math or playing chess suffers. What's lost is willingness; you would prefer to be asleep. You don't make errors of commission, but omission. . . . It's not your thinking or memory that goes—it's your will to go on."

Insomnia never kills a man until he kills himself.

—Axel Martin Munthe

Insomnia Is Kafkaesque

The bookshelves are filled with the works of authors who somehow kept composing despite harrowing nights. Just as art scholars wonder whether Goya's paintings take their dark and foreboding nuances from his vision problems, it is tempting to ponder how writers, always a bit on the edge, were influenced—or perhaps inspired—by sleep deprivation. Witness the diaries of Franz Kafka, the Czech writer who created such memorable alternative realities in works like "Metamorphosis" and "In the Penal Colony":

2 October 1911. Sleepless night. The third in a row. I fall asleep soundly, but after an hour I wake up, as though I had laid my head in the wrong hole. I am completely awake, have the feeling that I have not slept at all or only under a thin skin, have before me anew the labour of falling asleep and feel myself rejected by sleep. And for the rest of the night, until about five, thus it remains, so that indeed I sleep but at the same time vivid dreams keep me awake. I sleep alongside myself, so to speak, while I myself must struggle with dreams. About five the last trace of sleep is exhausted, I just dream, which is more exhausting than wakefulness. In short, I spend the whole night in that state in which a healthy person finds himself for a short time before really falling asleep. When I awaken, all the dreams are gathered about me, but I am careful not to reflect on them. Towards morning I sigh into the pillow because for this night all hope is gone

3 October 1911. To make myself as heavy as possible, which I consider good for falling asleep, I had crossed my arms and laid my hands on my shoulders, so that I lay there like a soldier with his pack. Again it was the power of my dreams, shining forth into wakefulness even before I fall asleep, which did not let me sleep.

15 November 1911. Yesterday evening, already with a sense of foreboding, pulled the cover off the bed, lay down, and again became aware of all my abilities as though I were holding them in my hand; they tightened my chest, they set my head on fire, for a short while, to console myself for not getting up to work, I repeated: "That's not healthy, that's not healthy," and with almost visible purpose tried to draw sleep over my head. I kept thinking of a cap with a visor which, to protect myself, I pulled down hard over my forehead.

21 November 1912. I lie here on the sofa, kicked out of the world, watching for the sleep that refuses to come and will only graze me when it does, my joints ache with fatigue, my dried-up body trembles toward its own destruction in turmoils of which I dare not become fully conscious. . . .

Tossing and Turning on Downing Street

Sometimes insomnia is more than a frustration—it's a political liability. One English prime minister of the past century, Archibald Primrose, Lord Rosebery, was compelled to resign his post because of his inability to get a good night's sleep. He wrote, "To lie, night after night, staring wide awake, hopeless of sleep, tormented in nerves and to realize all that was going on, at which I was present, so to speak, like a disembodied spirit, to watch one's own corpse, as it were, day after day, is an experience which no sane man with a conscience would repeat."

Winter Insomnia

The mind can't sleep, can only lie awake and
gorge, listening to the snow gather as
for some final assault.

It wishes Chekhov were here to minister
something—three drops of valerian, a glass
of rose water, anything, it wouldn't matter.

The mind would like to get out of here
onto the snow. It would like to run
with a pack of shaggy animals, all teeth,

under the moon, across the snow, leaving
no prints or spoor, nothing behind.
The mind is sick tonight.

—Raymond Carver

Vibration

The world vibrates, my sleepless nights
discovered. The air conditioner hummed,
I turned it off. The plumbing
in the next apartment sang;
I moved away, and found a town
whose factories shuddered as they worked
all night. The wires on the poles
outside my windows quivered in ecstasy
stretched thin between horizons.
I went to where no wires were; and there,
as I lay still, a dragon tremor
seized my darkened body, gnawed
my heart, and murmured, *I am you.*

—John Updike

The Rats Who Were Roused to Death

*It is for the doctors to decide whether sleep is such a necessity
that our very life depends on it.*

—Michel de Montaigne

Picture a laboratory full of caged rats. Each of their twitching little heads is wired to a brain-wave monitor, which is in turn linked to a mechanical contraption designed to wake them at the first sign of drowsiness. They can eat and drink as much as they like, but they can never sleep.

The first rat dies after thirteen days. Within twenty-one days, all are dead.

No, this is not a science-fiction sequel to *The Wind in the Willows*. It is a real-life experiment, renowned among sleep scientists, conducted by Dr. Allan Rechtschaffen at the University of Chicago. Rechtschaffen's results posed more questions than they answered—especially since postmortems on the rats revealed no apparent natural cause for death: no rapid onset of disease, no dramatic changes in organs or blood chemistry. The rats had simply been wakened to death.

Years later, a student of Rechtschaffen's shed more light on the mystery. After a series of similar tests, she concluded that her rats had died of bacterial infections of the blood—infections by microbes commonly found in every healthy rat. Apparently, the sleepless rats' immune systems had been so depressed that their most basic biological defenses had failed them.

Interestingly, humans deprived of sleep for extended periods—whether as volunteers in research projects, political prisoners under torture, or college students playing in marathon Monopoly tournaments—exhibit the same physical symptoms as the dying rats: disorientation, decreases in body temperature, and weight loss despite an ample or increased intake of food.

The moral of the story? Whether we court it or disdain it, sleep seems as essential to our survival as shelter, warmth, and food.

In Memoriam to Memory

To the casual observer, sleep may seem like a mindless state. But the sleeping brain is actually working hard at a vital clerical task: sorting and filing the day's experiences and moving them from short-term to long-term memory.

Like a computer sorting the day's files for backup in a searchable archive, long-term human memory is a miraculous thing: it's virtually limitless in capacity and relatively indestructible. Studies have shown, for example, that foreign words learned in a high school class and rarely used in daily life thereafter can be recalled fifty years later—provided the students slept well on the night in question.

How this manifests itself to sleep-starved insomniacs can be as trivial as forgetting an acquaintance's name or as profound as forgetting a lover's first kiss. What it means to our globally sleep-starved society is more troublesome. Medical students and residents, for example, must cram oceans of learning into near-impossible schedules, and the result can be misinterpreted data or missed diagnoses. And in Japan, ambitious students are expected to attend both regular schools and after-hours cramming schools called *juku*, then continue their diligent studying at night. As a result, they might pass the exams they need to secure good jobs, but they retain little of the knowledge—and display less of the creative thinking—required in day-to-day life on and off the job.

On the other hand, crafty mediators in protracted political and labor negotiations admit to using the lost-memory phenomenon to their advantage: as deadlines loom and the combative parties become increasingly tired, agreements are hammered out as once-crucial details simply slip from their minds.

Sleep-Deprived in Dresden

On the 1st of October 1893 I took up office as Setatsprasident to the Superior Court in Dresden. I have already mentioned the heavy burden of work I found there. I was driven, maybe by personal ambition, but certainly also in the interests of the office, to achieve first of all the necessary respect among my colleagues and others concerned with the Court (barristers, etc.) by unquestionable efficiency. The task was all the heavier and demanded all the more tact in my personal dealings with the members of the panel of five Judges over which I had to preside, as almost all of them were much senior to me (up to twenty years), and anyway they were much more intimately acquainted with the procedure of the Court, to which I was a newcomer. It thus happened that after a few weeks I had already overtaxed myself mentally. I started to sleep badly at the very moment when I was able to feel that I had largely mastered the difficulties of settling down in my new office and in my new residence, etc. I started taking sodium bromide. There was almost no opportunity for social distraction which would certainly have been very much better for me—this became evident to me when I slept considerably better after the only occasion on which we had been asked to a dinner party—but we hardly knew anybody in Dresden. The first really bad, that is to say almost sleepless nights, occurred in the last days of October or the first days of November. It was then that an extraordinary event occurred. During several nights when I could not get to sleep, a recurrent crackling noise in the wall of our bedroom became noticeable at shorter or longer intervals; time and again it woke me as I was about to go to sleep. Naturally we thought of a mouse although it was very extraordinary that a mouse should have found its way to the first floor of such a solidly built house. But having heard similar noises innumerable times since then, and still hearing them around me every day in daytime and at night, I have come to recognize them as undoubted divine miracles—they are called "interferences" by the voices talking to me—and I must at least suspect, without being too definite about it, that even then it was already a matter of such a miracle; in other words that right from the beginning the more or less definite intention existed to prevent my sleep and later my recovery from the illness resulting from the insomnia for a purpose which cannot at this stage be further specified.

My illness now began to assume a menacing character. . . .

—Daniel Paul Schreber, *Memoirs of My Nervous Illness*

Insomnia

The man goes to bed early but he cannot fall asleep. He turns and tosses. He twists the sheets. He lights a cigarette. He reads a bit. He puts out the light again. But he cannot sleep. At three in the morning he gets up. He calls on his friend next door and confides in him that he cannot sleep. He asks for advice. The friend suggests he take a walk and maybe he will tire himself out—then he should drink a cup of linden-tea and turn out the light. He does all these things but he does not manage to fall asleep. Again he gets up. This time he goes to see the doctor. As usual the doctor talks a good deal but in the end the man still cannot manage to sleep. At six in the morning he loads a revolver and blows out his brains. The man is dead but still he is unable to sleep. Insomnia is a very persistent thing. —Virgilio Piñera, "Insomnia," from *Cold Tales*

The Ordeal of Gilbert Pinfold

by Evelyn Waugh

I don't sleep naturally. I have tried everything—exercise, cold baths, fasting, feasting, solitude, society. Always I have to take paraldehyde and sodium amytal. My life is really too empty for a diarist. The morning post, the newspaper, the crossword, gin.

—Evelyn Waugh, *Diaries*

Mr. Pinfold also slept badly. It was a trouble of long standing. For twenty-five years he had used various sedatives, for the last ten years a single specific, chloral and bromide which, unknown to Dr. Drake, he bought on an old prescription in London. There were periods of literary composition when he would find the sentences he had written during the day running in his head, the words shifting and changing colour kaleidoscopically, so that he would again and again climb out of bed, pad down to the library, make a minute correction, return to his room, lie in the dark dazzled by the pattern of vocables until obliged once more to descend to the manuscript.

—Evelyn Waugh, *The Ordeal of Gilbert Pinfold*

In an example of art imitating life, *The Ordeal of Gilbert Pinfold* might just as easily be titled *The Ordeal of Evelyn Waugh*. Three years before writing it, the insomniac author suffered a terrifying spell of aural hallucinations and delusions of persecution resulting from a regimen of sleeping narcotics, rheumatism drugs, and alcohol. Aboard a ship bound for Ceylon, Waugh imagined outlandish threats and bizarre goings-on, and wrote in his diary of awakening thirty times per night to a cacophony of voices in his cabin, which he took "for other passengers whispering about me."

Waugh's alter ego, Gilbert Pinfold, is

a successful, middle-aged novelist who experiences similar side effects to medications as a passenger taking a recuperative cruise to Ceylon. No sooner does the gangplank lift than Pinfold hears sounds emanating from the ceiling of his cabin: wild jazz bands, barking dogs, religious revival meetings, a punitive clergyman, and voices ... talking about him:

All that evening, though there was an undertone in his ears, Mr. Pinfold was oblivious of the Angels. Not till late, when he was alone in his room, did the voices break through. "We heard you, Gilbert. You were lying to that American. You've never stayed at Rhinebeck. You've never heard of Magnasco. You don't know Osbert Sitwell."

"Oh God," said Mr. Pinfold, "how you bore me!"

Insomnia

directed by
Erik Skjoldbjaerg (1998)

Two detectives arrive in a remote town to unravel a mysterious murder. Only, the town is in northern Norway—the land of the midnight sun—and the region's thick mists and constant daylight lend an especially unnerving flavor to the classic film noir recipe. Early on, Jonas (Stellan Skarsgard), one of the detectives, commits an error that makes him complicit in the crime. He spends the rest of the investigation in a cold sweat, simultaneously protecting his secret, retaining his mask of professional detachment, and fighting a bad case of sleeplessness exacerbated by the never-ending days. When he accidentally kills his partner by shooting into a dense fog, Jonas is pushed to the breaking point.

rocket
fuel

Tempest in a Coffee Pot

The sleep-inhibiting—and heart-gladdening—effects of caffeine are so thirsted

after that virtually every culture on earth has devised some kind of caffeinated beverage. Chen Nung's paean to tea is one of the earliest known tributes, though there is evidence that Asians were boiling leaves centuries earlier.

By the sixth century, tea had spread to Japan, where Zen monks relied upon it to get through marathon meditation sessions. In the sixteenth century, the beverage was brought to Europe by returning Jesuit missionaries, and it had a profound effect on Western—and especially British—culture.

> ## It quenches thirst. It lessens the desire to sleep. It gladdens and cheers the heart.
> —Chinese emperor Chen Nung (attr.) in praise of tea, 2737 B.C.

Legend has it that coffee was discovered by an adventuresome ninth-century Middle Eastern goatherd who noticed his animals acting extra frisky, then bravely ingested the same berries they'd been gobbling. However discovered, and transformed from berry to beverage, coffee's fame soon spread through the Arab world; it was credited with boosting energy, battle skills, and sexual prowess. When Islamic ascetics condemned it as an intoxicant—and therefore banned by the Koran—hopped-up revisionists successfully argued that its mind-clearing qualities aided religious devotion. In the West, Roman Catholic Pope Clement VIII apparently agreed. As the drink made its way through Venice at the end of the sixteenth century, he was encouraged to ban it, but blessed it instead. Indeed, even today, Italians consume the beverage with almost religious fervor: there are approximately 150,000 coffee bars in Italy, and the population imbibes about 38 million *espressi* each day (tallying up to 14 billion per year).

Today, coffee ranks second only to water in worldwide consumption. Coffee's popularity is due in equal parts to flavor and chemistry: it not only tastes good, but its active ingredient, caffeine, is a quick-acting stimulant that delivers eye-opening neurological effects in mere minutes. Alas for insomniacs, it can take up to six hours—or as long as twenty-four hours in older people—for the body to rid itself of the drug. So indulge (sparingly) in the A.M., and after lunch stick to decaf—that brew of choice for fin de siècle overachievers.

Spark in a Bottle, Buzz in a Mug

Coca-Cola—a Southern concoction of kola-nut extract, sugar, and flavorings such as cinnamon, citrus, and vanilla—lost some of its punch after 1903, when cocaine was dropped from the top-secret recipe. But it kept its kick in the form of chemically pure caffeine. Initially promoted as a stimulant, Coke has been joined over the years by a host of uplifting soft drinks that contain anywhere from thirty-five to fifty-two milligrams of caffeine—about the same as a cup of tea.

Chocolate, too, is chock-full of stimulants, which explains, in part, why the "lulling cup of cocoa" is a myth. Researchers poking in cocoa cups have isolated a host of compounds that resemble those found in amphetamines, and which amp

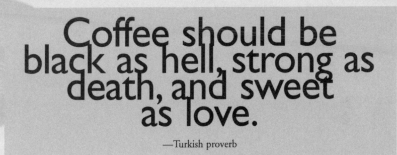

Coffee should be black as hell, strong as death, and sweet as love.
—Turkish proverb

up the caffeine that is also present. So, while a typical cup of cocoa contains around fifteen milligrams of caffeine, the effect is more like ingesting thirty. Less than a cup of coffee, but enough to keep the brain riffing at midnight.

All of which makes such elixirs questionable dinnertime beverages for insomniacs, children, or sleep-deprived new mothers, the latter of whom might perpetuate their own exhaustion by passing caffeine on to their nursing infants, who become bundles of boundless energy just as their moms are trying to unplug.

One evening, contrary to my custom, I drank black coffee and could not sleep. Ideas rose in crowds; I felt them collide until pairs interlocked, so to speak, making a stable combination. —Henri Poincaré, describing a moment of mathematical discovery

Balzac's Bitter Brew

Honoré de Balzac, the feisty French novelist, may never have written eighty-five novels in twenty years if not for his robust passion for coffee. Balzac died in 1850 at the age of fifty-one; the underlying cause, claimed his doctor, was "the use or rather the abuse of coffee, to which he had recourse in order to counteract man's natural propensity to sleep." The following is Balzac's last-ditch recommendation for defying sleep in favor of work:

Finally, I have discovered a horrible, rather brutal method that I recommend only to men of excessive vigor, men with thick black hair and skin covered with liver spots, men with big square hands and legs shaped like bowling pins. It is a question of using finely pulverized, dense coffee, cold and without water, consumed on an empty stomach. This coffee falls into your stomach, a sack whose velvety interior is lined with suckers and papillae. The coffee finds nothing else in the sack, and so it attacks these delicate and voluptuous linings; it acts like a food and demands digestive juices; it wrings and twists the stomach for these juices, appealing as a pythoness appeals to her god; it brutalizes these beautiful stomach linings as a wagon master abuses ponies; the plexus becomes inflamed; sparks shoot all the way up to the brain. From that moment on, everything becomes agitated. Ideas quick-march into motion like battalions of a grand army to its legendary fighting ground, and the battle rages. Memories charge in, bright flags on high; the cavalry of metaphor deploys with a magnificent gallop; the artillery of logic rushes up with clattering wagons and cartridges; on imagination's orders, sharpshooters sight and fire; forms and shapes and characters rear up; the paper is spread with ink—for the nightly labor begins and ends with torrents of this black water, as a battle opens and concludes with black powder.

—Honoré de Balzac, "Du Café"

The Caffeine Conundrum Most of us drink coffee in order to achieve what we consider to be a "normal" baseline of alertness—it helps us "be all that we can be." But Stanley Coren, author of the lively book *Sleep Thieves*, suggests otherwise. Citing studies that show that well-rested people do *not* experience enhanced performance after ingesting caffeine, he suggests that the morning (or midday) cappuccino does not increase alertness and competence as much as it corrects for an energy deficit caused by lack of adequate sleep. Which would help account for the ever-increasing popularity of caffeinated beverages (there are even caffeine-laced mineral waters on the market) and the fact that just about every business day, a new Starbucks opens its doors.

the enemy of sleep

of sleep

When the Brain Works Overtime

> ## He that thinks in his bed has a day without a night.
> —Scottish proverb

Insomnia has been called the "philosopher's disease"—an affliction of people whose love of thinking makes it particularly difficult to shut down the brain. And if an active mind guarantees wakefulness, those who try to think their way to unconsciousness are most doomed of all. For sleep, like sexual pleasure, is a goal most easily attained the less it is thought about. Trying to power your way to sleep is about as effective as having an orgasm on command—the effort itself sabotages the result.

Time-tested methods such as deep breathing, progressive relaxation, and counting sheep are all sound attempts to short-circuit the thought process in the hope of getting some shut-eye. But for the offspring of Western culture—philosophers or otherwise—obstacles are meant to be overcome, not surrendered to. And trying not to think is about as easy as determining the meaning of life.

Sleep is no servant of the will;
    It has caprices of its own:
When courted most it lingers still;
    When most pursued 'tis swiftly gone.
—Robert Browning

> ## To sleep means to disinterest oneself.
> ## We sleep in direct proportion to our disinterestedness.
> —Henri Bergson, *The Creative Mind*

For a long time I used to go to bed early. . . . And half an hour later the thought that it was time to go to sleep would awaken me.
—Marcel Proust, *Swann's Way*

The Crowded Head of Charles Dickens

Perhaps, with no scientific intention or invention, I was illustrating the Duality of the Brain; perhaps one part of my brain, being wakeful, sat up to watch the other part which was sleepy. Be that as it may, something in me was as desirous to go to sleep as it possibly could be, but something else in me *would not* go to sleep, and was as obstinate as George the Third.

Thinking of George the Third—for I devote this paper to my train of thoughts as I lay awake: most people lying awake sometimes, and having some interest in this subject—put me in mind of Benjamin Franklin, and so Benjamin Franklin's paper on the art of procuring pleasant dreams, which would seem necessarily to include the art of going to sleep, came into my head. Now, as I often used to read that paper when I was a very small boy, and as I recollect everything I read then as perfectly as I forget everything I read now, I quoted "Get out of bed, beat up and turn your pillow, shake the bed-clothes well with at least twenty shakes, then throw the bed open and leave it to cool; in the meanwhile, continuing undrest, walk about your chamber. When you begin to feel the cold air unpleasant, then return to your bed, and you will soon fall asleep, and your sleep will be sweet and pleasant." Not a bit of it! I performed the whole ceremony, and if it were possible for me to be more saucer-eyed than I was before, that was the only result that came of it. . . .

I had proceeded thus far, when I found I had been lying awake so long that the very dead began to wake too, and to crowd into my thoughts most sorrowfully. Therefore, I resolved to lie awake no more, but to get up and go out for a night walk—which resolution was an acceptable relief to me, as I dare say it may prove now to a great many more.

> The mind, everyone's mind, is forever unstill, is a continual restlessness like light, even in sleep, when the light is inside and not outside the skull.
>
> —Harold Brodkey, "Dying: An Update"

In the bar he was always tired, and he sometimes fell asleep standing up, with open eyes. The brilliant light and the noises made his head swim. But as he walked home from the Grand Hotel after midnight the cold air revived him so that he entered his small room wide awake. This he knew to be a dangerous hour. If now a thing caught his mind it would stick in it with unnatural vividness and keep him from sleep, and he would be no good for his books the next day. He promised himself not to read at this time, and while he undressed to go to bed he closed his eyes.

—Isak Dinesen, "The Fat Man"

TO ACHIEVE THE IMPOSSIBLE DREAM, TRY GOING TO SLEEP.

—Joan Klempner

Once, in Florence, I suffered an extended—that is, roughly two-week—bout of insomnia, not at all helped by a too soft bed and an almost continuous flow of motor-scooter traffic vrooming past my hotel window. I tried to concentrate on pleasant things: small animals I have loved, tennis courts in the rain, giraffes cantering off into the distance. None of it worked. All I was finally left to think about was the longing for sleep itself—a topic always guaranteed to keep one awake.

—Joseph Epstein, "The Art of the Nap"

I can't sleep; no light burns;

All round, darkness, irksome sleep.

Only the monotonous

Ticking of the clock,

The old wives' chatter of fate,

Trembling of the sleeping night,

Mouse-like scurrying of life . . .

Why do you disturb me?

What do you mean, tedious whispers?

Is it the day I have wasted

Reproaching me or murmuring?

What do you want from me?

—Alexander Pushkin, "Lines Written at Night During Insomnia"

Mulla Naṣrudin was walking through the streets at midnight. The watchman asked, "What are you doing out so late, Mulla?" "My sleep has disappeared and I'm looking for it."

—Idries Shah

Sleep was growing more and more improbable, the losing side of a debate. Imagine a happy thing. Imagine yourself comfortable and at home and your body will step through that narrowing door. Imagine sleep as a door to step through, a field to fall in, a treetop to rock in, a chair to sink in, a hammock to swing in, a car to ride in, a horse to sit on. I could have slept if it rained.

—Robert Glück, *Jack the Modernist*

Rosie

by Anne Lamott

I'm not a good sleeper. It's just part of my nature. I can't seem to change it; like I can't change the color of my eyes.

Lithe, elegant, literate, and affluent Elizabeth Ferguson is the widowed mother of Rosie, a precocious girl with deep-blue Siamese-cat eyes. As her daughter goes through the rites of passage of childhood, Elizabeth struggles to find a purpose in life, to choose a suitable partner, and with the growing pains of motherhood—all excellent fodder for her invisible demon, insomnia.

Elizabeth's days are filled with reading, cooking, avoiding social encounters, and thinking about drinking. Her nights are suffused with scotch, brandy, and sleeplessness. Anyone who has ever passed the night endlessly awaiting—and dreading—the alarm clock will find her internal monologue hauntingly familiar:

It was one-fifteen by the luminous clock; if she fell asleep soon she could still get almost six hours' sleep before she had to get Rosie up for school.

If you fall asleep right now, you can still get five and a half hours. She turned the light back on, picked up the book, but couldn't concentrate.

If you fall asleep _now_, you can still get five....

If you fall asleep right _now_, you can still get four hours and forty minutes of sleep.

The pillow was hot and scratchy, and she turned it over, resting her face on the cool cotton. The sheets itched, felt as sandy as her eyes, and she flopped around the bed. She hugged a pillow, one end between her legs: her teddy bear, her lover. Four hours would be fine.

The Insomniac's
Film Festival

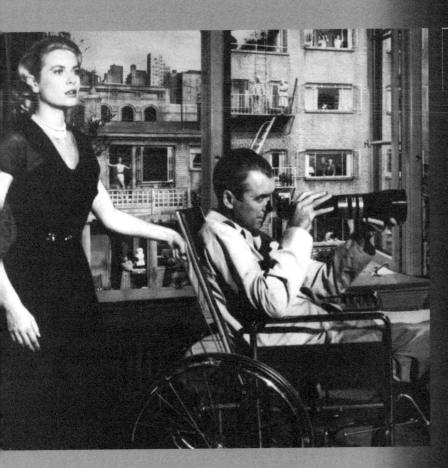

Rear Window

directed by

Alfred Hitchcock (1954)

Wheelchair-bound by a broken leg, action photographer Jeff Jeffries (James Stewart) is plagued by itches he can't scratch. Cooped up in his apartment, he eases his cabin fever by observing his neighbors—and divining their life stories—through a telephoto lens. Gradually, Jeffries begins to suspect that the salesman in the opposite apartment is up to no good. Why has his invalid wife disappeared from her bed? What's he been doing with the knives and the saw that he cleans at the kitchen sink? Where does he go on those postmidnight forays with his weighty sample case? As Jeffries spends night after sleepless night trying to unravel the mystery, his voyeurism turns from amusement to obsession—and eventually puts his own life at risk.

dead men waking

Maladies from the Fatal to the Merely Frightful

Don't go to sleep—so

As if chronic sleep loss were not disabling enough, imagine knowing that the condition was not only permanent, but terminal.

Welcome to the world of fatal familial insomnia (FFI). Like kuru ("laughing cannibal disease") and the infamous mad-cow disease, FFI is a spongiform encephalopathy, which in layman's terms means it turns your brain into something resembling a hunk of swiss cheese.

If recent Nobel Prize–winning theories are to be believed (and some scientists don't believe them), FFI is caused by proteins called prions that somehow switch between two shapes. One is common and perfectly harmless, the other—the first's mirror image—is deadly. The renegade proteins link together in chains that surround and strangle nerve cells, leaving holes in brain tissue that lead to loss of motor control, dementia, paralysis, and, eventually, death.

In FFI, this process is probably a result of hereditary genetic factors. The symptoms include a gradual decline in REM sleep, followed by a lack of sleep altogether. The victim literally dies of progressive—and irreversible—sleep deprivation.

Because the disease is so rare (no more than a few dozen verified cases have cropped up worldwide) it is often mis- or undiagnosed. One music teacher in the Chicago area, for example, was told by doctors that he had multiple sclerosis, then was committed to a mental institution for severe depression, before a correct diagnosis was made.

Three weeks later, he died.

many people die there.

—Mark Twain

The Last Gasp If you're like most people, you've had the experience of being startled awake with the anxious feeling that you've stopped breathing. Often the cause is innocuous: perhaps you're simply emerging from that recurring dream about being full-nelsoned by your former gym teacher. Or maybe you've just been kicked awake by a bedmate who can't tolerate your snoring.

For an estimated 10 percent of men and 4 percent of women, snoring is the first warning sign of a risky disorder called sleep apnea. Apnea occurs in several forms, but all include a momentary yet complete halt in breathing caused by blockages in the airway. In some cases, respiratory interruptions can occur once per minute, with the frequent wakings and associated anxiety leading to a nasty case of insomnia.

A further complication: When we sleep, our brains switch to a kind of neurological autopilot, and various bodily functions—among them the maintenance of vital oxygen levels in the blood—are monitored less closely. Combine this with a bad case of sleep apnea, and blood oxygen levels can plummet to hazardously low levels, resulting in desperate fatigue, damage to cells in the brain and nervous system, long-term problems including high blood pressure and heart disease, and perhaps even asphyxiation. (And there are other risks: infamous outlaw John Wesley Hardin reportedly once became so enraged with a snorer in a neighboring room, he shot the man to death!)

Most common in middle-aged men who've put on a few too many pounds, mild apnea can sometimes be controlled by losing weight, avoiding nightcaps and nicotine, and sleeping on the belly. Chronic sufferers may resort to wearing a mask attached to an air pump, or, in more desperate cases, a number of surgical procedures—including one grisly option that involves removing, then reattaching, the tongue.

The Horizontal *Danse Macabre*

Wherefore to some, when being a Bed they betaken themselves to sleep, presently in the Arms and Leggs, Leapings and Contractions of the Tendons, and so great a Restlessness and Tossings of their Members ensue, that the diseased are no more able to sleep, than if they were in a Place of the greatest Torture.

—Thomas Willis, M.D., *The London Practice of Physick* (1685)

The good doctor Willis made these poignant observations in the seventeenth century, but it took the medical establishment almost three hundred years to peg the disorder with a moniker: PLMS, or period leg movements during sleep. Whether you know it or not, it could be the physiological cause of your insomnia.

The marionette-like dance of PLMS becomes more prevalent as we age, and eventually affects more than 40 percent of people over sixty-five. Afflicted souls suffer involuntary, herky-jerky movements every thirty seconds or so. The average attack lasts for several hours, and severe cases can last all night. As a result, sleepers put up with hundreds of brief awakenings, which play havoc with the duration and quality of their slumber.

A rarer form of the disorder is even more debilitating. Victims of restless leg syndrome feel as if hundreds of ants are scurrying inside their calves or shocks of electricity are shooting through their legs, often in addition to the spastic thrashing of PLMS. Sometimes it's nearly impossible for the poor devils to sit or lie still—and sleep is out of the question.

Out Like a Light

Every thousandth person you meet suffers from a hereditary neurological condition called narcolepsy—insomnia's evil twin. Its victims experience daytime sleep attacks that can send them to dreamland in mid-sentence, at a meeting, or while driving across a crowded boulevard. The results—ranging from embarrassment to death—must be dealt with every day, as the ailment is treatable (with drugs that can have dangerous side effects) but not curable. One famous sufferer, the American essayist Henry David Thoreau, felt "it was a daily triumph just to stay awake until nightfall." Another, Quentin Crisp, found humor in his situation: "I sleep in the cinema, at the theater, in my room while watching television, or indeed anytime that I am not walking about. Perhaps that is why I have lived so long—and why I don't rule the world."

What Flavor Is Your Insomnia?

Seek treatment for your wakefulness and you're likely to be asked what type of insomniac you are: sleep onset, middle, or early A.M. How you respond will likely determine your treatment.

It takes the average good sleeper from eight to fifteen minutes to fall asleep, but chronic sufferers of sleep-onset insomnia may take three times as long. Interestingly, both good and bad sleepers tend to exaggerate this "sleep-onset latency" period. Middle (or maintenance) insomnia often strikes following the first complete sleep cycle (about two hours after falling asleep), and can recur throughout the night, resulting in a colossal sleep debt by morning. Frequently induced by misuse of sleep medication or alcohol, this type of insomnia is most easily treated. Waiting like a serpent in the grass is early A.M. insomnia, which can be a symptom of depression—especially depression triggered by an emotional loss—as well as sensitivity to light or noise.

If you're afflicted by any of these types of insomnia, take heart: some lucky folks experience all three.

sleep hygiene:
the
brutal
truth

Sage Advice and Sad Reality

The good people sleep much better at night than the bad people.

Of course, the bad people enjoy the waking hours much more.

—Woody Allen

Self-help books and magazine articles are rife with "simple tips" for beating insomnia. But unless you've recently joined an ascetic religious order, the cure can be as burdensome as the malady:

The Rule
Minimize your caffeine intake, and under no circumstances drink coffee within six hours of bedtime.

The Reality
The proposal is due tomorrow morning, and it's already 7:15 P.M. Are you going to reach for a refreshing Perrier or a triple espresso?

Alcohol can help make you drowsy, but it disrupts refreshing deep sleep and dream sleep. Take it easy with the booze, and don't drink anything within two hours of hitting the hay.

When you finally print out the proposal at 11:45 P.M., are you going to celebrate with a tall glass of milk or a double martini with extra olives?

Avoid arguments and other anxiety-inducing traumas before bedtime.

When you crawl into bed at 2:00 A.M., reeking of gin, your bedmate throws a screaming fit and insists on talking about it *now*.

If you smoke, stop. Nicotine is a stimulant, and nonsmokers sleep more easily than smokers.

Quitting smoking is among the most stressful experiences known to humankind and will probably wreak havoc with your sleep patterns.

The Rule

Make sure your bedroom is quiet and dark. If you need to, invest in a soothing "white noise" machine, or wear earplugs and a sleep mask.

Keep your bedroom cool—between 50° and 75° F. As you fall asleep, your body temperature starts to drop, and excessive warmth can be disruptive.

Schedule a relaxing wind-down period every evening before bed. Complete all personal and work-related business beforehand, and spend a couple of hours reading or watching TV.

Regular aerobic exercise is essential. But be sure to do it at the right time: morning exercise does not help induce sleep, and a workout within three hours of bedtime may overstimulate you.

Avoid heavy meals within four hours of bedtime. The digestive process stimulates your body in ways that decrease your ability to sleep soundly.

The Reality

Earplugs only increase the volume of your internal demons' voices and may cause you to miss a fire alarm and die of smoke inhalation. The sleep mask makes you look like Tallulah Bankhead on a bad day.

The steam heat in your apartment is haphazardly controlled by an absentee landlord. The radiators hiss and clank at inopportune hours of the early morning. If you shut them off, you will freeze to death.

Pagers, e-mail, voice mail, the global economy. Your only bedside reading is a book your boss gave you for your birthday: *Taking Advantage of the Twenty-four-Hour Business Cycle.* Every morning he quizzes you on his favorite chapters.

The only time you can make it to the gym is before even the most ambitious Starbucks is open, or after prime time—when you are least motivated to go, and the sleep benefits are dubious.

After grabbing a stale doughnut for breakfast and inhaling half a sandwich at your desk for lunch, a leisurely evening meal is one of the last great pleasures in life. But by the time you drag yourself to the gym and get home, it's at least nine o'clock—and you use your remaining energy to order a large pepperoni pizza.

The Rule
If you *do* wake up in the middle of the night, don't look at the clock. It will only increase your anxiety and make it difficult to fall asleep again.

Above all, keep regular hours. Ben Franklin's dictum of "early to bed, early to rise" has been confirmed by numerous sleep researchers.

The Reality
Whenever your eyes pop open, they naturally gravitate to the glowing green numerals. If you've turned the clock to face the wall, trying to guess the time is more stressful than just getting it over with.

Get a life, Ben.

The Pause That Refreshes

When Americans travel the world—especially to Mediterranean countries and other temperate zones—they invariably encounter a local custom that leaves them somewhere between puzzled and annoyed. Tanked up on espresso, guidebooks in hand, they are shocked to encounter shuttered windows, abandoned streets, and a communal yawn in the postlunch hours. For their part, the locals can't imagine why these foreigners are so antsy.

The siesta is a centuries-old tradition in dozens of cultures, where only "mad dogs and Englishmen go out in the midday sun." But this venerable custom is increasingly knuckling under to the demands of a sleep-disdaining world—for reasons ranging from global economic priorities to local traffic management.

Yet even in places where the siesta is not an established custom, many will attest to the usefulness, or at least harmlessness, of the occasional midday nap. Artists from da Vinci to Dalí and world leaders from Charlemagne to Churchill, for example, have been champion catnappers—with nothing but salutary effects on their work and productivity. Modern-day sleep gurus are divided on the benefits of napping, however. Some say it can put a crimp on a good night's rest. But others, such as Harvard sleep physiologist Martin Moore-Ede, believe that we are biologically programmed for naps, that they are a time-effective way to redress sleep deficits and enhance productivity. Moore-Ede even helps companies set up employee nap rooms, where those who toil long hours can take a break—and presumably awake refreshed, energized, and ready to tackle tasks that would otherwise fall prey to fatigue.

The Pause That Saves Lives Although pilot fatigue is a well-known occupational hazard that has led to tragedy, most airlines have been loathe to incorporate scheduled pilot and copilot naps into their flight plans. However, since a NASA study on planned naps in the cockpit demonstrated marked improvement in both pilot alertness (16 percent improved reaction time) and performance (34 percent decline in lapses of awareness), several nondomestic airlines have adopted the sensible practice. Alas, the nap stigma has prevented any domestic carriers from following suit—forcing pilots flying for these airlines to continue to grab their forty winks "off the record" (and occasionally at the same time as their weary copilots).

one sleeps, the other doesn't

And Other Grounds for Divorce

There is a gulf fixed between those who sleep and those who cannot. It is one of the greatest divisions of the human race.

—Iris Murdoch, *Nuns and Soldiers*

"Opposites attract," goes the old chestnut. Its veracity is still hotly debated in women's fashion journals and men's lifestyle magazines, where an equal number of articles support the theory as refute it. But when it comes to sleep habits, there seems to be some truth in the statement. Often, a weak sleeper will find herself hooked up with a maestro of slumber—or vice versa.

It's obvious why nature abhors insomniac couples: the odds are that one will be murmuring the familiar "Are you awake?" just as the other has finally nodded off—only to be returned the favor a few hours later. It's doubtful that anyone would ever get any shut-eye.

The mating of two hearty sleepers seems more effective on the surface, but might be less so from a Darwinian standpoint. For ever-vigilant insomniacs are expert detectors of the noises psychotic killers might make, should they care to intrude. And someone has to stay awake to wonder if the door is really locked, whether the smoke alarm has any batteries, and if the cat will succumb to distemper if she stays out all night.

A Woman's Rest Is Never Done

If you're blessed with two X chromosomes, you are twice as likely as a man to seek

help for insomnia (even factoring for his innate stoicism). Your fluctuating proges-

terone levels create a biochemical circus with any number of hormonal sideshows.

The menstrual cycle, pregnancy, and menopause—with its attendant hot flashes—can

all wreak havoc with a woman's rest. Something to remember the next time his love-

making coda consists of a good snooze while you feel ever more alert and awake.

I have always wondered why the fact that men have to sleep has never been really utilized by women, who are basically insomniac, when men transgress. Why have men never intuited that sleeping next to a woman you abuse all day might be hazardous? Drifting off I got into a fantasy of haranguing some feminist friends of mine with: Men sleep! We don't! Power is lying in the street and nobody bothers to pick it up!

—Norman Rush, *Mating*

I know what sleep's supposed to look like. It's what happens to my wife each night: She crawls under the covers, fluffs her pillow just right and in moments, drowsy bliss comes bounding to her like a faithful St. Bernard. But sleep for me is a wayward thing, more like an indifferent feline who curls up on my chest only when it suits her.

Even when I do nod off, my slumber is shallow and unrefreshing. I sleep in fits and starts. I have disconcerting dreams that leave me frazzled and out of sorts. I wake achy and wasted to stumble fuzzy-headed through my days. It takes me three tries, minimum, to dial long-distance. I can't remember names. I drink washtubs full of coffee. I look like hell.

—Vince Rause, "One Man's Quest for a Good Night's Sleep"

I would steal an hour of my lover's sleep if I could. I would slip beneath his eyelids and yank it right out of him. He would feel nothing. Nor would I—neither remorse nor shame. One hour of perfect unconsciousness: one clean, soundless dive, deeper and deeper, as far as my lungs would take me. I would come up for air before he woke. Instead, I lie motionless, sewn to the sheets by the smallest demons, watching Steve's silhouette against the bedroom blinds. Fondness becomes hostility. How does he do this for eight hours? I listen to his tranquil breathing, furious that he sleeps while I cannot.

—Bill Hayes, *Sleep Disturbances*

In the dead of night wives talked to their husbands, in the dark they talked and talked while the clock on the bureau ticked sleep away, and the last street cars clanged off on distant streets to remoter suburbs, where in new houses bursting with mortgages and the latest conveniences wives talked in the dark, and talked and talked. All over the country the wives' voices droned on and on about the bridge prizes, the luncheon, the hollandaise sauce, the walnut surprise, the little defeats, the little jealousies, the children, the grocer, the neighbor, and husbands might put pillows over their heads or stuff their ears with cotton, pretend to snore, sigh loudly with fatigue, no matter, the voices went on and on, riveting the darkness, hammering into the night hush, as ceaselessly and as involuntarily as cricket noises.

—Dawn Powell, *Angels on Toast*

Sleep waits in its velvet dress,
the nightbirds grieve, the dark lawn
stretches into dogwood trees. My wife

breathes slowly through her mouth, blue sheet
gathered at pale breasts. The telephone
rests in its hard bed, the dog dreams,

the house ticks and sighs. All day long,
all night the steel rain, but now
it stops. Small water

ticks from spatulated leaves. The planet
turns, my wife turns. Sleep lies between us
like an old love, longed for in the dark.

—Jon Loomis, "Insomnia"

The Stilly Night: A Soporific Reflection

He unwinds himself from the bedclothes each morn and

        piteously proclaims that he didn't sleep a wink, and

        she gives him a glance savage and murderous

And replies that it was she who didn't close an eye until

        cockcrow because of his swinish slumber as evi-

        denced by his snores continuous and stertorous,

And his indignation is unconcealed,

He says she must have dreamed that one up during her

        night-long sweet repose, which he was fully con-

        scious of because for eight solid hours he had listened

        to her breathing not quite so gentle as a

        zephyr on a flowery field.

The fact is that she did awaken twice for brief intervals

        and he was indeed asleep and snoring, and he did

        awaken similarly and she was indeed unconscious

        and breathing miscellaneously,

But they were never both awake simultaneously.

Oh, sleep it is a blessed thing, but not to those wakeful

        ones who watch their mates luxuriating in it when

        they feel that their own is sorely in arrears.

I am certain that the first words of the Sleeping Beauty

        to her prince were, "You *would* have to kiss me just

        when I had dropped off after tossing and turning for

        a hundred years."

—Ogden Nash

Lark or Owl: It's in the Genes

Larks (people who spring from bed in the A.M. with the enthusiasm of Olympic gymnasts) often feel morally superior to Owls (the party animals who have energy to burn at midnight but can barely muster the effort to slam the snooze bar the next morning). But rather than being a mark of virtue, the ability to be bubbly in the morning is most likely a question of ancestry. Research by Stanford University sleep expert Emmanuel Mignot suggests that a mutation on chromosome 4—the clock gene—plays a large role in determining a preference for morning or evening activity. Which doesn't really help if you're late for work or your partner sleeps through your amorous advances, but might make you feel better anyway.

I cannot sleep. My insomnia is a kind of gay and lively palpitation, and I sense in your immobility the same quivering exhaustion. You do not budge. You hope I am asleep. Your arm tightens at times around me, out of tender habit, and your charming feet clasp mine between them. . . . Sleep approaches, grazes me, and flees . . . I can see it!

—Colette, *Earthly Paradise: An Autobiography*

Sleepless in Seattle

directed by

Nora Ephron (1993)

Sam Baldwin (Tom Hanks) is a recently widowed Seattle architect with a bad case of melancholic insomnia. He's been mourning his wife for so long that his precocious son, Jonah, decides to take matters into his eight-year-old hands. Jonah phones a late-night radio talk show to broadcast a plea: he wants a new wife for his grieving Dad. When the talk-show host bullies Sam onto the airwaves for a bittersweet description of his lost love, at least one listener is moved to tears. She's Annie Reed (Meg Ryan), a recently engaged Baltimore journalist who finds in "Sleepless in Seattle's" anonymous voice all the romance that's missing in her fiancé. When Annie responds with a letter, the comedy of errors begins, with Jonah conspiring to bring the two together and dozens of circumstances conspiring to keep them apart.

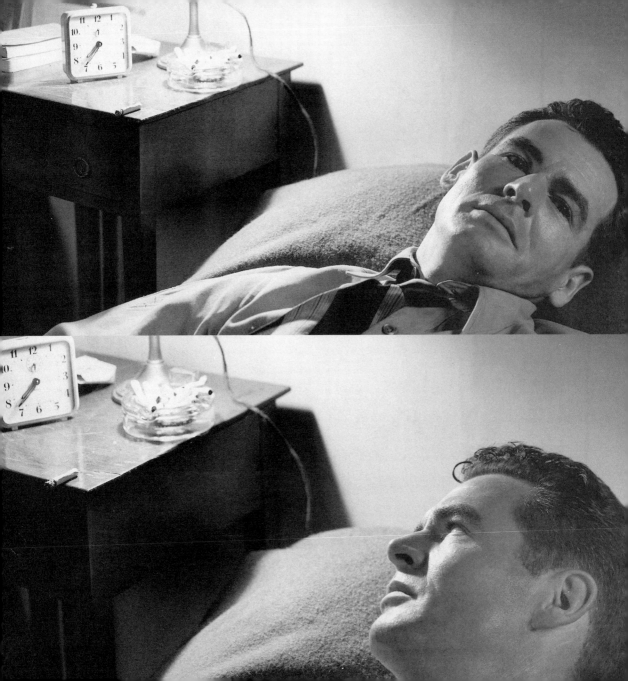

the loneliest club on earth

Confederacy of the Comatose

I am just like many more
Who lie in bed, still and numb
Awake enough that I can see
Just how dark it has become.

—Joe Henry, "King's Highway"

To be awake in the dead of night is to come face to face with a blank wall of solitude. Lying alone and apart from the dozing crowd, James Thurber empathized with the similarly stricken: "I dread, as much as anyone else, the white watches of the woeful night, but, unlike most of my insomniac friends and enemies, I often think of the thousands of others who are also lying awake." Lonesome insomniacs have a meager selection of venues in which to seek human company. A glowing diner on an otherwise darkened street, a bar just before closing time, an all-night truck stop, or a 'round-the-clock Laundromat or copy shop can, in the hours before dawn, become an unofficial clubhouse for the dazed and dreamless.

What's the matter with me?
I don't have much to say
Daylight's sneaking through the window
And I'm still in this all-night café.

—Bob Dylan, "Watching the River Flow"

The Congress of the Insomniacs

Mother of God, everyone is invited:
Stargazing Peruvian shepherds,
Old men on sidewalks of New York.
You, too, doll with eyes open
Listening to the rain next to a sleeping child.

A big hotel ballroom with mirrors on every side.
Think about it as you lie in the dark.
Angels on its ornate ceilings,
Naked nymphs in what must be paradise.

There's a stage, a lecture,
An usher with a flashlight.
Someone will address this gathering yet
From his bed of nails.
Sleeplessness is like metaphysics.
Be there.

—Charles Simic, *Hotel Insomnia*

The thing about insomnia is that you do it alone. Yet it comforts me to think I am in good company, one among the confederacy of the sleepless. . . . Now when I awaken at some empty hour, I imagine an art dealer I know across town doing crossword puzzles in the bathroom, using his girlfriend's eyeliner as a pencil; my friend Anne brewing an inky black sleep potion purchased in Chinatown; and, out in Brooklyn, Gregory lying in bed listening to the all-night *Larry King Live* on headphones, so as not to wake his wife.

—Lois Nesbitt, *Mirabella* magazine

The dimensions of night—night time, night space—seem larger: the crowds are thinner, the pace is slower, the parking easier. And after a certain point of no return, people even become friendlier, maybe because they are fewer, maybe because insomniacs have a freemasonry of their own and there is a companionship in being up and about while the rest of the world sleeps.

—A. Alvarez, *Night*

How to deal with these hours,

alone under the ceiling's black canopy

while the clock multiplies its two fingers

into ten, eleven, twelve,

cracks its knuckles at midnight,

builds an exclamation point,

then starts all over again?

—Adrien Stoutenburg, "Midnight Saving Time"

—Lie down in sleep but suddenly
this windowless bathroom?
white-glaring tiles? porcelain
sink so fiercely scoured
it's dancing with flames?
and no shadowy corners?
and the chrome faucets
too hot to touch? and
the perfect pool of the toilet
bowl in which a single eyeball
floats? and the mirror
so polished there's nothing
beyond the surface not even
you?

—Joyce Carol Oates, "Insomnia"

things to do when the sun don't shine

Channeling Your Wee-Hour Energy

I'll go to sleep if I can; if I cannot, I'll rail against all the first-born of Egypt.

—Shakespeare, *As You Like It*

I sit up half the night playing records when I have the blues and can't get drunk enough to get sleepy.

—Raymond Chandler

Here you are again. Wide awake at an unconscionable hour, vulnerable to what Roger Angell calls a "fetid blast of night thoughts." You *could* sink into a familiar stew of remorse—or you might try to distract your brain with less self-destructive activities.

Instead of alphabetizing your CDs (by artist? by title?), sorting your closet (by color? by season?), or having a go at the bathroom grout, some experts advise that it's best to stay in bed and wait for sleep to wash over you like a balm. The following suggestions are culled from a few wide-eyed scribes who've come to terms with their excess of early-morning hours. And all can be done flat on the back, without moving a muscle.

James Thurber Profoundly Ponders the Letter "P"

For those watchers of the night who wake at the old Scott Fitzgerald hour and know darn well they are not going to get to sleep again, I suggest a ramble, a fascinating safari, through one of the letters of the alphabet....

The letter "P," that broad, provocative expanse between "O" and "Q," is one of the most ambivalent of all the twenty-six, for in it one finds pleasure and pain, peace and pandemonium, prosperity and poverty, power and pusillanimity, plethora and paucity, pornography and prudery, purity and prurience, public and private, pastime and punishment, the patrician and the proletarian, and on and on, words without end....

The experienced souse will not linger long in a letter that serves little more than punch, porter, Pernod, pop, Pepsi, Dr. Pepper, Pilsner, Peruna, pousse-café, and—but our souse has already staggered on to the stronger drinks of "R" and "S" and "W," waving aside the philtre that makes a person philous, for sex is not his weakness, and for him Philomela plays her lyre of gold in vain....

What has kept me awake most recently are the wonderful pixies of "P," major and minor, immortal and ephemeral—and, my God, are they plentiful: Puck, Punch, Punchinello, Pinocchio, Pan, Peter Pan, the Pied Piper, Peter Piper, Prunella, Pierrot and Pierette, Prancer, Pogo, Penrod, Mary Poppins, Joe Palooka, the Pimpernel, Prospero, Pollyanna, Peg o' My Heart, Puss in Boots, Pooh, the Pod (out of *Sybil's Garden of Pleasant Beasts,* and if you have a copy you're lucky), Popeye (the sailor-man, not the Faulkner fiend), Peck (the naughty son of old man Peck, not Gregory), Pluto (Disney's dizzy dog), and Paddock (the frog friend of the witches in *Macbeth*)....

Prisoners of parody and paraphrase, prostrate and pillowed, are prone to tinker with the world and words of Lewis Carroll at the slightest prod or provocation. And so my very latest nights have been plagued by persistent poppycockalorum like this: "'Twas throllog and the siren tones did shriek and gibber in the night, all menace were the bomberdrones, and the mom wrath outright." But enough of this, and, if you should ever be able to fall asleep at night from now on, pleasant dreams.

—James Thurber, "The Watchers of the Night"

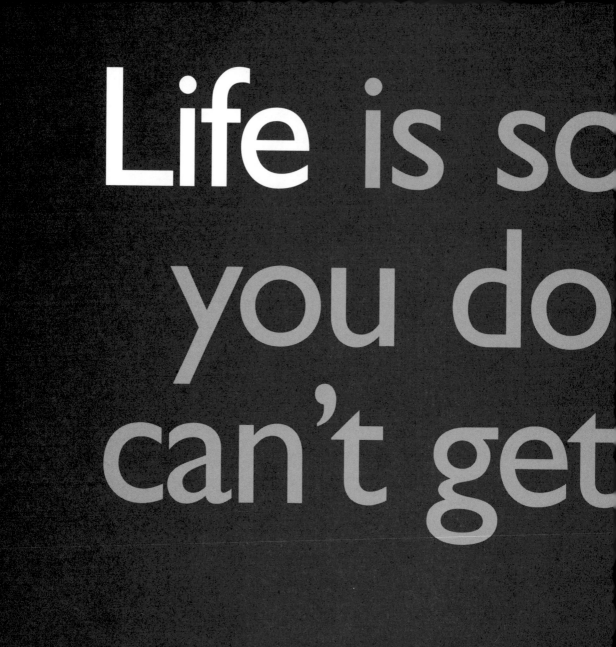

Life is so
you do
can't get

mething
when you
to sleep.

—Fran Lebowitz

Jean Kerr's Epistolary Exercises

Lately I find that just as I am sinking into that first sweet slumber of the night I suddenly remember I forgot to take a leg of lamb out of the freezer. At this point I have two clear alternatives. I can pad down to the garage and get the lamb, or I can lie there and figure out what else we could have for dinner tomorrow night (hamburger, or what our five-year-old calls "creamed chipped beast").

Either way I'm fully awake now, bright-eyed, alert. Indeed there seems to be a penetrating sharpness to my mind, a quickness that I never notice in the daytime. At this moment I feel that I could be profitably reading Toynbee's *A Study of History* or the directions on the Waring blender.

The problem is, of course, to channel this alarming mental energy before I lapse back into that old, and disastrous, habit of reviewing the low points of my life (the night I swallowed an inlay in the Oak Room at the Plaza, the day I dropped—and smashed—a large bottle of mineral oil in the elevator of the Time-Life Building, the Sunday that Honey, our cocker spaniel, ate my mother-in-law's wristwatch).

It was only recently that I discovered that one could put this otherwise lost time to work and make it pay off in terms of mental health, which, I am sure we are all agreed, becomes more elusive all the time. Now I just make a list of all the tiny irritations that have been nibbling away at my subconscious, and I compose dignified letters of protest. (Major irritations, like plumbers who come and make extensive repairs on the wrong bathtub and dry cleaners who press boys' jackets without removing the chocolate kisses from the pockets, I omit on the theory that these really require a stern phone call.) I find that after I have written one of these letters mentally I forget the whole matter and the next day my mind is clear to grapple with real problems, like where on earth I put all those Halloween costumes last November.

And, actually, these nocturnal doodlings hurt nobody. I never do type them up in the morning because I'm too sluggish and, on the various occasions when I suggested that I might really mail one of them, my husband has always stopped me by asking a simple question: "Are you out of your mind?"

I am putting down a few sample letters here in case there is another insomniac who would like to be as disagreeable as possible (without repercussions) but hasn't quite got the hang of it. . . .

The Ever-Krisp Curtain Co.

Dear Sirs:

In what mad burst of whimsy did you adopt the slogan "These curtains laugh at soap and water"? Now, I begrudge no man his flights of fancy. We are all poets at heart. And when I purchased my Ever-Krisp curtains I did not really expect them to burst into wild guffaws or even ladylike giggles the first time I put them in the sink. (As a matter of fact, with five small boys and one loud Siamese cat I don't want to hear one word from those curtains.) But, in my incurable naïveté, I did take your claim to imply that these curtains actually survived contact with soap and water. I don't mean I expect them to remain ever-krisp. I'm quite accustomed to ever-limp curtains. I did, however, expect them to remain ever-red with ever-white ruffles. As it happens, they are now a sort of off-pink strawberry ripple, which of course doesn't go with my kitchen.

Ever Disgusted

Dear Sister Saint Joseph:

Colin tells me that he is playing the part of the Steering Wheel in the Safety play. He feels, as do I, that he could bring a lot more to the part of the Stop Sign. I know Stop Sign is a speaking part, and while I realize that Colin is not ready for "leads," still he did memorize all three stanzas of "America, the Beautiful," and I myself would have absolute confidence in his ability to handle the line "I am the Stop Sign, and I am here to help you," which I understand constitutes the whole part. Also, Colin is very tall for seven and I'm sure we're agreed that height is very important for this role. Finally, let me mention (although I do not expect it to influence your decision in any way) that I just happen to have a Stop Sign costume which I made for his brother three years ago.

Cordially,

Colin's Mother

Dear Doctor Lipman:

Those new sleeping pills that you said would "fell an ox" don't work either. Now what will I do?

Desperately,

Jean

—Jean Kerr, "Letters of Protest I Never Sent"

Lewis Carroll's Conundrums

Most celebrated as the author of *Alice's Adventures in Wonderland* and *Through the Looking-Glass*, Lewis Carroll (Charles Dodgson) was also an Oxford mathematics lecturer who nursed a life-long love of acrostics, word games, and puzzles. His "calming calculations" offer alternatives to "the harassing thoughts that are apt to invade a wholly-unoccupied mind."

Given that the brain is in so wakeful a condition that do what I will, I am certain to remain awake for the next hour or so, I must choose between two courses, viz. either to submit to the fruitless self-torture of going through some worrying topic, over and over again, or else to dictate to myself some topic sufficiently absorbing to keep the worry at bay. A mathematical problem *is*, for me, such a topic; and is a benefit, even if it lengthens the wakeful period a little. I believe that an hour of calculation is much better for me than half-an-hour of worry.

—Lewis Carroll, "Pillow Problems Thought Out During Sleepless Nights"

Into the Night

directed by

John Landis (1985)

Something is gnawing at aerospace engineer Ed Okin (Jeff Goldblum). Despite all the trappings of a solid middle-class life—loving wife, good job, a peppy car to fight the Los Angeles traffic—he's spent a month's worth of nights staring at the bedroom ceiling. When the effects of sleep deprivation take a toll on his work, he heads home for a daytime nap, only to find his wife in bed with another man. Ed does an about-face, gets in his car, and drives—aimlessly, then unwittingly into a madcap adventure involving foreign agents, huge sums of money, a beautiful young woman (Michelle Pfeiffer), and, at long last, a good night's rest.

the curse of the water nymph—
and other harrowing tales

Revenge Strategies with a Twist

May your bed sprout onions.

—Yiddish Curse

Once upon a time, a stunning water nymph named Ondine fell in love with a brutally handsome knight named Sir Lawrence. So deep was her love, the watery wench was willing to sacrifice her immortality in order to marry him. Their vows were poignant and heartfelt: "My every waking breath shall be my pledge of love and faithfulness to you," swore Sir Lawrence. "As long as our love is true, my magic will serve as your shield and will never be turned against you," promised Ondine.

So much for prenuptial agreements.

After giving birth to a son, Ondine's magical beauty began to fade. A sag here, a crow's foot there, and Sir Lawrence's eye began to wander. One afternoon, from behind a barn door, she heard him snoring and followed the familiar sound to find him naked in the hayloft—with a local trollop in his arms. Quivering with rage and mourning all she had given up for him—beauty, immortality, the works—Ondine pointed a bewitching finger and made her husband's prophetic words haunt him forever: "You swore faithfulness with every waking breath. Should you ever fall asleep again, then that breath will be taken, and you will die!"

Interestingly, before medical parlance became less poetic and more politically correct, sleep apnea—the dangerous condition that interrupts a sleeping person's breathing—was known as Ondine's curse.

Live!

It's easy to say. If at least I could work up a little interest in living—but I'm too tired to make the effort. Since you left me, Ondine, all the things my body did by itself, it now only does by special order . . .

I have to supervise five senses, two hundred bones, a thousand muscles. A single moment of inattention, and I forget to breathe. He died, they will say, because it was a nuisance to breathe.

—Jean Giraudoux, *Ondine*

If anyone lays his hands
on my tomb
and opens my grave,
I pray to the gods
of the netherworld that
his soul shall roam
in the scorching sun
after death....
Let the ghost of
insomnia take hold
of him for ever and ever.

—Eighth-century B.C. curse found on a tomb in the ancient city of Nimrud,
the military capital of the Assyrian kingdom

When I lie down, I say, When shall I arise, and the night be gone?
And I am full of tossings to and fro unto the dawning of the day.

O cruel Love, on thee I lay

My curse, which shall strike blind the day:

Never may sleep with velvet hand

Charm thine eyes with sacred wand . . .

The bed thou liest on be despair;

Thy sleep, fond dreams; thy dreams, long care;

Hope (like thy fool) at thy bed's head

Mock thee, till madness strike thee dead.

—John Lyly, "Sappho and Phao"

Methought I heard a voice cry, "Sleep no more!
Macbeth does murder sleep"—the innocent sleep,
Sleep that knits up the ravell'd sleeve of care,
The death of each day's life, sore labour's bath,
Balm of hurt minds, great nature's second course,
Chief nourisher in life's feast. . . .
Still it cried, "Sleep no more!" to all the house:
"Glamis hath murder'd sleep, and therefore Cawdor
Shall sleep no more; Macbeth shall sleep no more."

—Shakespeare, *Macbeth*

**Pity us!
Oh pity us!
We wakeful.**

—Rudyard Kipling

soporifics, from A to Z

A Potpourri of Ways to Seduce Sleep

Halfway through my life, I still wander at night. I still seek the peerless soporific. Everybody has a cure to recommend, whether it's warm milk, frisky sex, or melatonin. One friend solemnly prescribes whiffing dirty socks before turning out the lights. I find, though, that home remedies are no more effective than aphrodisiacs. Sleeping pills can force the body into unconsciousness, it's true. I have had my jags on Halcion and Xanax, Ambien and Restoril. I've slept many times on those delicious, light-blue pillows. But the body is never really tricked. The difference between drugged and natural sleep eventually reveals itself, like the difference between an affair and true romance. It shows up in your eyes. Sleep acts, in this regard, more like an emotion than a bodily function. As with desire, it cannot be pursued. Sleep must overtake you. —Bill Hayes, *Sleep Disturbances*

Acupuncture. The insertion of needles along carefully selected meridians of the body has been used in China since ancient times to help restore the flow of *chi*—vital energy—in the treatment of a wide range of ailments, including insomnia.

Alcohol. Hot toddy, nightcap, warm brandy: just the ticket for a comforting night's sleep? Biochemically, alcohol is a central-nervous-system depressant—which would seem to support the notion that a late-night nip will ease the journey to dreamland. But in reality, imbibing alcoholic beverages close to bedtime is more of a snake in the grass: it can reduce REM sleep in the initial hours, triggering an increase in REM later in the night, and this "REM rebound" often results in intense dreams, nightmares, and premature awakenings—and an inability to fall back to sleep.

Apple, daily. To cure his insomnia and regularize his habits, the French writer Alexandre Dumas (of *Three Musketeers* fame) made it a point to eat an apple every morning at seven beneath the Arc de Triomphe.

Aspirin. Widespread anecdotal evidence suggests that two aspirin at bedtime may help prolong the time spent asleep and thus encourage a feeling of being well rested the next morning. Take with a full glass of water—or, even better, a mug of warm milk.

Bath, hot. A good long soak can relax your muscles, ease tension, and put you in a more meditative frame of mind. And moving from bath to bed begins a gradual cooling process which is normally associated with dozing off.

Biofeedback. The "mind over body" technique was developed in the 1950s, partially in response to reports of Zen masters and Indian yogis who could voluntarily control bodily functions long considered to be purely involuntary—slowing the metabolic rate, decreasing oxygen consumption, raising and lowering body temperature. Research eventually confirmed—first with monkeys and then with humans—the viability of the "relaxation response" mastered by these mystics, and the biofeedback industry was born. To condition their relaxation responses, most people are trained with an inexpensive device that measures such things as breathing, pulse rate, and muscle tension. Often used in conjunction with visualization exercises, biofeedback can teach people to relax deeply—sometimes a critical step toward conquering insomnia.

Bedroom, restricted-use

Many sleep savants believe that your bedroom should be a shrine for only two activities, sleep and sex. For this reason, they say, boudoir lighting should be lulling, pillows inviting, noise kept at bay, and anything (except the alarm clock) related to daily stresses should be banished. The psychological logic is sound: if you use your bed for reading, eating, working, and telephoning, it may lose its magical association with sleep.

There are, of course, those who defied this advice with remarkable success. Marcel Proust wrote in bed, perhaps because his constitution was too weak to leave it. Mark Twain was a robust fellow, but he, too, chose to do his work horizontally—probably to enhance the glee of knowing that, as long as he pleased himself and his readers, no man was his boss. And Samuel Beckett did most of his writing between the sheets, in the process producing literature's most singular string of paralytic protagonists.

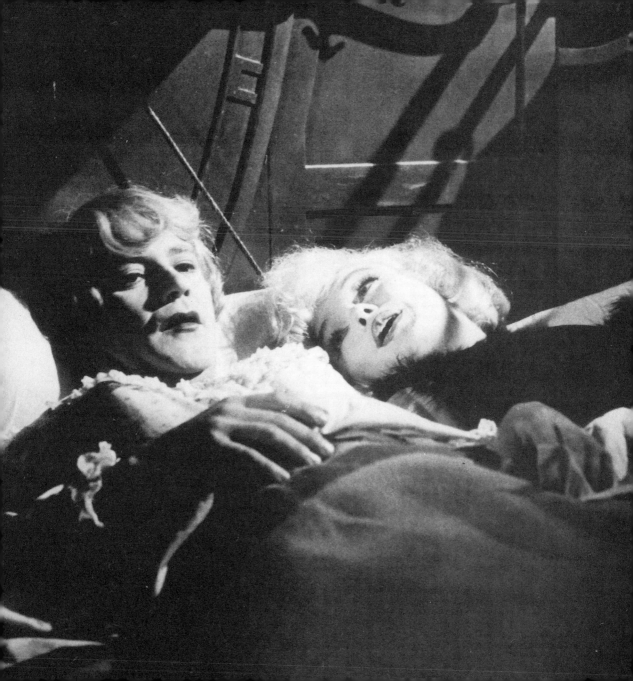

Bedtime stories

For some people, a tedious book is all it takes to make the lids grow heavy and the hand grope for the bedside light. Writing about his own literary remedies for seducing sleep, Roger Angell describes his "little shelf  of classical pharmacopoeia." Happily, all of these authors are readily available over the counter: "George Eliot, James, and Montaigne are Nembutals, slow-acting but surefire. Thoreau, a dangerous Seconal-Demerol bomb, is reserved for emergencies; thirty minutes in the Walden beanfield sends me back to bed at a half run, fighting unconsciousness all the way down the hall."

Camphor. "I treat my insomnia with a very strong dose of camphor in my pillow and mattress," wrote Vincent van Gogh. This from a man who painted some of art history's most spectral images, lopped off his ear for love, and shot himself at age thirty-seven.

Catnip. A favorite mind-altering substance of felines, it turns out that people have drunk *Nepeta cataria* as a tea for centuries, to help calm the mind and encourage sleep. No placebo effect, it is now known that cis-trans-nepetalactone—the volatile oil's major component—resembles the chemical structure of the valepotriates, the natural sedatives found in valerian.

Chamomile. A popular postprandial infusion for those who shun coffee, chamomile contains a volatile oil that has been shown to have a mild depressant effect on the central nervous system. In dispute is whether chamomile tea offers enough of the oil to be effective; some herbalists cite beneficial cumulative effects. The flowers themselves are an excellent soporific, and can be tossed into a warm bath to enhance relaxation.

Counting. Sheep. Friends. Enemies. Past lovers. Slights. Mortifications. Years gone by . . .

Deep breathing. The deep, from-the-diaphragm breath associated with yoga practice and meditation can help clear the mind and release the body with its slow, almost hypnotic inhalation and exhalation. Start low in the abdomen and expand the chest slowly on the inhale, reverse the process by forcing air out with the abdomen on the exhale. And try not to let the mind wander.

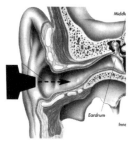

Earplugs. It's no secret that noise can keep you from dozing. But it may also yank you from deeper to shallower phases of sleep, resulting in loss of quality as well as quantity of sleep. For obvious reasons, earplugs are best-sellers in nearly every corner deli in New York.

Exercise. Staying fit has innumerable health benefits, including a better sleep life. But take care to work out three to five hours before retiring. Otherwise your postgym energy buzz and elevated body temperature can inhibit sleep.

Golf, mental. A certain New York publisher induces sleep by conjuring the world's great golf courses and playing the holes stroke by stroke in his mind. He rarely makes it to the ninth, and has yet to walk the entire course (or match his nighttime score during daylight hours).

Food, gourmet

The Physiology of Taste, Jean-Anthelme Brillat-Savarin's witty and erudite meditations on the art of eating well—and living well—has been in continuous print since its appearance in 1825, the year before its author's death. This self-published encyclopedic masterpiece, the result of some thirty years of research, addresses every possible topic relating to food, including its effects on sleep and dreams:

He has eaten wisely, though refusing neither good nor excellent cheer; he has drunk the best wines, and, albeit cautiously, even the most famous. At dessert his talk has been gallant rather than political, and he has made more madrigals than epigrams; he has drunk a cup of coffee, if it agrees with his constitution, and accepted a few moments later a spoonful of excellent liqueur, simply to sweeten his mouth. In all things he has shown himself a charming guest, a distinguished connoisseur; and yet he has only barely exceeded the limits of necessity.

Under these circumstances he goes to bed content with himself and the rest of the world; his eyes close; he passes through the twilight zone, and then falls fast asleep. . . .

Soon Nature has levied her tribute, and his losses are repaired by assimilation. Then sweet dreams provide him with a mysterious existence; he sees those he loves, resumes his favourite occupations, and is wafted to those places where he has known happiness.

At last, he feels sleep gradually dispelled, and returns to social life with no reason to regret wasted time, because even in sleep he has enjoyed activity without fatigue and pleasure unalloyed.

Homeopathy. Because homeopaths approach the whole individual, rather than a specific symptom, insomnia treatments vary according to the person and the root cause of the condition. Homeopathic remedies include aconite (for fear-induced insomnia), arnica (for extreme fatigue), coffea (to calm a racing mind), phosphorus (to counteract night terrors), ignatia (to quell the obsession that you will never sleep again), and nux vomica (for insomnia caused by excessive drinking).

Hop. Known as "the flower of restful sleep," the herb has been used to flavor beer since the ninth century, when it was observed that hop pickers fatigued easily. A common ingredient in over-the-counter sleep aids, in 1983 hop was scrutinized by scientists, who isolated 2-methyl-3-butene-2 oil—which accounts for its sedative properties. Because of alcohol's interference with sleep patterns, hop is best taken as a tea, or added to a bath.

Hypnosis. Entering a hypnotic trance enables you to tap into your subconscious (in a way that resembles dreaming) while retaining awareness of the external world. Bypassing the ingrained habits of your conscious mind, hypnotic suggestions may, indeed, help change the behaviors and alleviate the stresses that cause chronic insomnia. But hypnosis is not for everyone: subjects who are most suggestible enjoy the greatest success.

Kava. The South Pacific herb (known also as kava kava) has a growing legion of enthusiasts who use it to reduce anxiety and restlessness and to facilitate sleep "naturally." Compounds found in the root and stem of the plant have muscle-relaxing and anticonvulsant effects.

Lavender. With its spare, clean scent, long prized by perfumers, lavender's aromatherapeutic properties are enjoying a renaissance. In one English experiment, for instance, researchers found marked improvement among chronic insomniacs when drugs were withdrawn and essence of lavender oil diffused into the air. In another study, chemist Leopold Jirovetz at the University of Vienna released the fragrance into a cage of mice, who soon began to doze. After the fragrance was cut off, the rodents resumed their scampering. Still, while lavender can induce a feeling of drowsy calm, Jirovetz advises that "it's not possible to inhale enough to put a person completely to sleep."

Lemon balm. Used like a mild form of Valium in centuries past, lemon balm was well known in the Middle East as well as Europe. Arab physicians prescribed it, while Charlemagne ordered the perennial to be grown in all of the medicinal herb gardens in his domain. And the famous seventeenth-century British herbalist Thomas Colepeper observed that it "driveth away all troublesome cares and thoughts out of the mind, arising from melancholy and black choler." More modern studies have shown that the herb has a sedative effect on the central nervous systems

of lab mice. People tend to drink it as a tea, or stuff it into pillows (*see* sleep pillows).

Marijuana. In 1894, the India Hemp Commission listed among marijuana's benefits the reduction of anxiety and the prevention of insomnia. Recent Western studies, however, indicate that regular use can interfere with sleep and increase anxious feelings. But results are mixed: in 1969, one sleep lab reported that marijuana reduced REM sleep; a year later, another lab claimed the opposite effect. Most casual users agree on the herb's sleep- and dream-inducing qualities—but like any psychoactive compound, its effects vary widely according to time and frequency of use, potency of dose, and the smoker's own mental state.

Massage. Many believe that the benefits of working out the kinks carry over into the night. Others find that while it's easy to fall asleep on the massage table, it's harder to recapture the bliss later on, after the world has intruded.

Mattress, well maintained

This bed was invented by others; know we go
to sleep less to rest than to participate
in the orthic twists of another world.

—John Updike, from "Tossing and Turning"

Though entire cultures once swayed to sleep on hammocks strung between trees, and 1970s couples swung (and sometimes even slept) on vinyl beds filled with water, the Better Sleep Council still heartily recommends that old standby, the coil-spring mattress.

Prolonging the life of your mattress is as simple as flipping and rotating it four times a year. But intermittent insomnia can be a clue that it's time to put the old friend out to pasture. After about eight to ten years, most mattresses will develop sagging spots, discomfort zones, odd creaks and crunches—which can lead to interrupted sleep and sore or stiff muscles.

But never fear: mattress-testing is one of the most enjoyable types of shopping there is. Look for a model at least seven inches thick, with a minimum of three hundred coils for a full-size, three hundred seventy-five for a queen, and four hundred fifty for a king. Space-age materials enable new mattresses to be supportive without feeling rock-hard; still, you should roam the showroom and audition each model, making sure that your shoulders, hips, and lower back don't sink too low.

Meditation. Pick a mantra, any mantra. It can be the single syllable *om* rising from your diaphragm; it can be the name of your third-grade teacher, repeated ad infinitum until it loses all meaning. Whatever it is, though, the purpose of the exercise is to keep your brain from thinking thoughts, any thoughts. The goal is stillness . . . stasis . . . peace . . . sleep.

Melatonin. A hormone produced in the pineal gland in the center of the brain, melatonin caused a stampede to health-food stores in the mid-1990s, when it was touted as nature's own cure for insomnia, jet lag, winter blues, and even as an inhibitor of the aging process. Whatever its other benefits, melatonin is known to be a regulator of the sleep/wake cycle, and recent research suggests that it is beneficial in preventing insomnia, especially in older people who've lost their ability to produce it naturally. Many people use it as a safer alternative to prescription sleeping aids, but its reputation as a magical cure-all is still a matter of debate.

Music. Babies seem to find lullabies a relaxing way to drift off—or maybe it's just that parents enjoy having an outlet for their musical talents and babies just fall asleep easily. In any case, some people find that a little night music can be an effective bridge from waking to sleeping—as long as you're not worried about turning off the stereo.

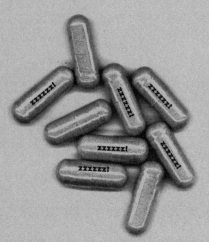

Over-the-counter sleep aids. Most of those pills with the cutesy names are really antihistamines in disguise, their sedative properties just a side effect. Like prescription drugs, they tend to lose their effectiveness with regular use and should be taken sparingly. Some may cause fatigue, or even agitation, the following day.

Passionflower. Recognized as a sedative for centuries by South Americans, and brewed by early Native Americans into a nerve-calming tea, passionflower contains potent tranquilizing chemicals (maltol, ethyl-maltol, and flavonoids). While not recognized officially in the United States as either safe or soporific, passionflower is a common ingredient in many sedative concoctions overseas.

Pharmaceuticals

He is immune to pills: red, purple, blue—

How they lit the tedium of the protracted evening!

Those sugary planets whose influence won for him

A life baptized in no-life for a while,

And the sweet, drugged waking of a forgetful baby.

Now the pills are worn-out and silly, like classical gods.

Their poppy-sleepy colors do him no good

—Sylvia Plath, "Insomniac"

Most insomniacs never confess their troubles to their doctor. Of those who do, two-thirds are pre-scribed sleeping pills, a circumstance that has created a $15 billion-a-year industry. Once gobbled like breath mints at a junior prom, sleeping pills are now dispensed a bit more selectively and for shorter periods. The reasons: they tend to lose their effectiveness rather quickly—within weeks or, at most, months—and they are addictive: once you've developed a tolerance for a sleep drug, your sleeplessness can become worse if you stop using it—a phenomenon called rebound insomnia.

Popular in the early twentieth century, barbiturates (Amytal, Nembutal, Seconal, Tuinal) are more quickly addictive than more recent sleep-inducing drugs, and feature more dangerous side effects—including highly disturbing dreams. Mixing them with alcohol can be fatal (witness Marilyn Monroe), making the combination a popular method of bloodless suicide.

Benzodiazepines, or antianxiety drugs, include Ativan, Dalmane, Halcion, Librium, Restoril, and Valium. While they are less likely than other sedatives to have dangerous side effects, they can cause depressed breathing and, over time, dependence and diminished memory. Halcion has even been outlawed in some countries, after having been linked to violent crimes and suicides.

The latest group of short-acting sleeping pills, including Ambien and Sonata, don't interfere with deep sleep and are said to pose less risk of daytime grogginess than their predecessors. But some diehard insomniacs find that their three- to four-hour effectiveness is not quite enough to get them through the night.

Pictures

One Rx for sleep, circa 1939:

Pictures in the bedroom should be suggestive of repose and tranquility. Do not make your bedroom a picture gallery. Two, or at the utmost three, fine prints suggestive of some pleasant scene in life are all that are needed. The author also traced several cases of insomnia to bloodcurdling prints. In one case of a mismated couple the sight of the marriage license framed in red caused the wife's insomnia. "I cannot sleep," she told me, "with the signs of calamity hanging over my head." —Maurice Chideckel, M.D., *Sleep Your Life's One-Third*

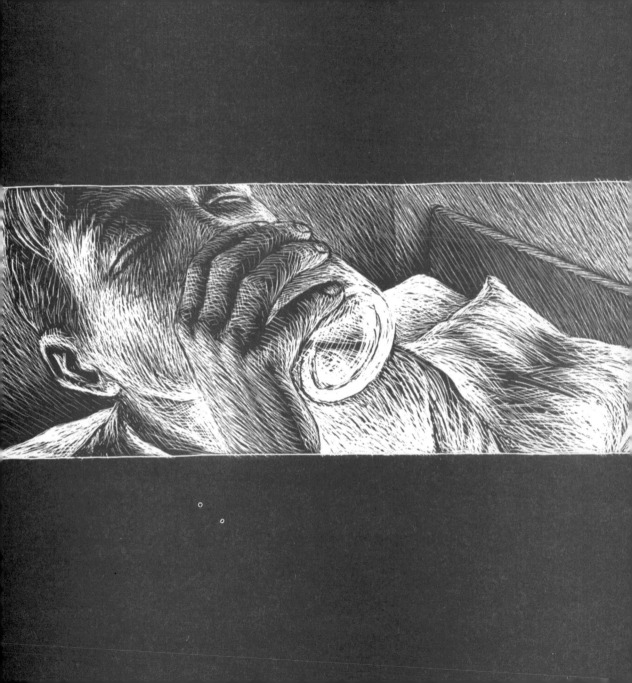

Pillows, perfect. "Fatigue is the best pillow," crowed Benjamin Franklin, but he died long before foam rubber came into use. Most people agree that down offers the optimal blend of softness and support, but if you find yourself sniffling at night, you might be allergic to feathers and should opt for foam. Above all, don't prop your neck up too high; it can force your spine into an unnatural curve. A common mistake among pillow buyers is choosing a big pillow that's good for reading, rather than a flatter one more suited to sleeping.

Proust, Marcel, *Remembrance of Things Past.*

"Nearly midnight. The hour when an invalid, who has been obliged to set out on a journey and to sleep in a strange hotel, awakened by a sudden spasm, sees with glad relief a streak of daylight showing under his door. Thank God, it is morning! The servants will be about in a minute: he can ring, and some one will come to look after him. The thought of being assuaged gives him strength to endure his pain. He is certain he heard footsteps: they come nearer, and then die away. The ray of light beneath his door is extinguished. It is midnight; someone has just turned down the gas; the last servant has gone to bed, and he must lie all night in agony with no one to bring him relief."

Perhaps the world's most prolific insomniac, Marcel Proust dedicated his life to writing about his alter ego, whose problematic relationship with sleep is introduced in the opening paragraphs of *Swann's Way,* the first book of the monumental *Remembrance of Things Past.* Soon thereafter, in a bedtime encounter between Marcel and his parents, the author establishes a critical theme: Marcel's use of his insomnia to attain that which he most desires—his mother's undivided attention and complete devotion.

"My aching heart was soothed; I let myself be borne upon the current of this gentle night on which I had my mother by my side. I knew that such a night could not be repeated; that the strongest desire I had in the world, namely to keep my mother in my room through the sad hours of darkness, ran too much counter to general requirements and to the wishes of others. . . . To-morrow night my anguish would return and Mamma would not stay by my side."

Today, public opinion varies on whether or not Proust's interminable oeuvre is itself a riveting saga or a potent (if nonaddictive) soporific.

Rituals

The history of human sleep is rife with eccentric fads, rites, and notions. One local legend among San Franciscans is that of a man who spent a half hour each night in his wife's bed, but could only fall asleep in the open coffin that he kept in an adjoining room.

Benjamin Franklin, who believed (long before medical science concurred) that heat was an enemy of sleep, kept two beds in his freezing-cold room and moved to the second as soon as the first became warm. The biographer Thomas Boswell mentions a certain British lord who awoke promptly at four A.M. each night to throw open a bedroom window and embrace a blast of chill night air—the better to appreciate the relative coziness of his bed. Like Franklin, Winston Churchill was another who favored dual beds—to relish the joy of moving to a fresh, unwrinkled resting place halfway through the night.

Long before *feng shui* came into vogue in the West, Charles Dickens habitually carried a pocket compass on his travels, to ensure that his bed was aligned on a north-south axis. He believed that magnetic currents coursing between the poles would benefit him if they flowed straight through his body.

Isolated in the chilly north of England, and subject to the constrained lives of minister's daughters, the sleepless Brontë sisters, Charlotte and Emily, walked in endless circles around the dining-room table, plotting out their novels until succumbing to exhaustion. When Charlotte's insomnia was exacerbated by grief after Emily's death, her friend and biographer Elizabeth Gaskell reports that "this was the time for the last surviving sister to walk alone, from old accustomed habit, round and round the desolate room, thinking sadly upon the 'days that were no more.'"

Sex, good. Note: the bad kind may induce a state of greater wakefulness.

Skullcap. Popular in ancient China and nineteenth-century America, this flower's merits as a sleep tonic continue to be debated. Some vociferously extol its virtues as an antidote to restlessness, excitability, tension, hysteria, night terrors, and agitation, and claim that it helps ease withdrawal from addictive drugs.

Sleep pillows. Flowers and floral sachets are an ancient folk cure for insomnia; Cleopatra is said to have slept on a rose-filled pillow, and both Abraham Lincoln and King George reputedly laid their heads on pillows filled with hops. Today, as insomnia assumes epidemic proportions, so-called sleep pillows abound in health-food stores and bed-and-bath shops. Lavender, hops, and lemon balm are just a few of the herbs commonly placed under the head to encourage sweet dreams.

Tryptophan. An amino acid found in cheese, milk, and meat, tryptophan is used by the body to make serotonin, a sleep-inducing chemical in the brain. Many studies have shown that a gram or two can be an effective antidote to mild insomnia. Once available in health-food stores, tryptophan was removed from shelves in 1989, when a contaminated batch was linked to the deaths of at least thirty-eight people. It is now available by prescription only. Milk, however, is naturally rich in tryptophan, which might explain the popularity of the warm-milk nightcap.

Valerian. The Pied Piper may well have used more than mere music to lure the children of Hamelin away in a hypnotic trance. Valerian, an herb that intoxicates cats and attracts rats, also has a sedative effect on humans. Today, more than one hundred drugs based on valerian and its derivatives are marketed in West Germany alone. While such pharmaceuticals are unavailable in the United States, the fresh rootstock can be made into a bitter tea or found in herbal bath concoctions.

Variations, Goldberg. Johann Sebastian Bach's Goldberg Variations—a collection of thirty devilishly difficult variations on a theme (which catapulted pianist Glenn Gould to fame)—were composed in 1742, in part to ease the insomnia of a well-heeled aristocrat.

White noise. Simulating sounds as varied as the surf, the wind, rainfall, and a porpoise's plaintive cry, bedside sound machines help induce sleep by masking intrusive noises with continuous background noise. Some doctors maintain that tuning a radio to the static between FM stations will work just as well.

Yoga. Thousands of years of meditative breathing and stretching practice have perfected a tech-

nique that lulls some into a state of deep serenity, and helps alleviate maladies such as anxiety, high blood pressure, and premenstrual syndrome. For others, however, the mere thought of standing on one's head is enough to derail sleep.

You've got to tell me, brave captain
Why are the wicked so strong?
How do the angels get to sleep
When the devil leaves his porch light on?

—Tom Waits, "Mr. Siegel"

Sleep-Related Organizations

American Sleep Apnea Association

A nonprofit organization dedicated to reducing injury, disability, and death from sleep apnea and to enhancing the well-being of those affected by this common disorder. Promotes education and awareness, research, and continuous improvement of care, and maintains a network of voluntary mutual support groups.

American Sleep Apnea Association
1424 K Street NW, Suite 302
Washington, DC 20005
tel: (202) 293-3650
fax: (202) 293-3656
www.sleepapnea.org

The Lucidity Institute

Dedicated to the advancement of research on the nature and potential of consciousness and to the application of the results of this research to the enhancement of human health and well-being.

The Lucidity Institute
2555 Park Boulevard, Suite 2
Palo Alto, CA 94306-1919
tel: (800) GO-LUCID (465-8243), or (650) 321-9969
fax: (650) 321-9967
www.lucidity.com

Narcolepsy Network

A national, nonprofit organization; members are people who have narcolepsy (or related sleep disorders), their families and friends, and professionals involved in treatment, research, and public education regarding narcolepsy.

Narcolepsy Network
P.O. Box 42460
Cincinnati, OH 45242
tel: (513) 891-9936
www.websciences.org/narnet

National Center on Sleep Disorders Research

A federal agency whose mission is to support research, scientist training, the dissemination of health information, and other activities with respect to sleep disorders and sleep-related research.

National Center on Sleep Disorders Research
c/o National Heart, Lung and Blood Institute
31 Center Drive, Room 4A11 MSC 2490
Bethesda, MD 20892-2490
tel: (301) 496-7443
fax: (301) 402-8307

Restless Legs Syndrome Foundation

A nonprofit agency that provides information about RLS; helps develop support groups; supports research to find better treatments and, eventually, a definitive cure; educates physicians and patients about RLS; and publishes a quarterly newsletter entitled *NightWalkers*.

Restless Legs Syndrome Foundation
4410 19th Street NW Suite 201
Rochester, MN 55901-6624
www.rls.org/main.asp

Sleep/Wake Disorders Canada

A national voluntary organization dedicated to helping people suffering from sleep/wake disorders by distributing information, encouraging research, establishing self-help groups, and acting as an advocate when necessary.

Sleep/Wake Disorders Canada
3080 Yonge Street, Suite 5055
Toronto, Ontario M4N 3N1 CANADA
tel: (416) 483-9654
fax: (416) 483-7081
www.geocities.com/HotSprings/1837

On the Internet

American Sleep Disorders Association (ASDA) Home Page

The ASDA is a professional medical association representing practitioners of sleep medicine and sleep research. Site offers links to accredited sleep clinics across the country.
www.asda.org

The Association for the Study of Dreams

A nonprofit, international, multidisciplinary organization dedicated to the pure and applied investigation of dreams and dreaming.
www.asdreams.org

Phantom Sleep Page

Resources to help people understand, identify, and overcome sleep apnea, snoring, and other sleep disorders.
www.newtechpub.com/phantom/index.html

Sleep Home Pages: Brain Information Service

The University of California, Los Angeles, School of Medicine's doorway to all things sleep-related.
bisleep.medsch.ucla.edu

Sleep Medicine Home Page

Resources regarding all aspects of sleep, including the physiology of sleep, clinical sleep medicine, sleep research, federal and state information, patient information, and business-related groups.
www.users.cloud9.net/~thorpy

SleepNet

Everything you wanted to know about sleep disorders but were too tired to ask.
www.sleepnet.com

The Sleep Well

A reservoir of information on sleep, sleep disorders, and sleep-related events. Compiled under the auspices of Dr. William Dement, the dean of American sleep researchers.
www.stanford.edu/~dement

Usenet Discussion Group

Contact, query, and share support and advice with other sleepless souls.
alt.support.sleep-disorder

Suggested Reading

A. Alvarez, *Night: Night Life, Night Language, Sleep, and Dreams* (New York: W. W. Norton, 1995).

Richard M. Coleman, *Wide Awake at 3 A.M.* (New York: W. H. Freeman, 1986).

Stanley Coren, *Sleep Thieves* (New York: Free Press, 1995).

William C. Dement and Christopher Vaughan, *The Promise of Sleep* (New York: Delacorte, 1999).

Lydia Dotto, *Losing Sleep* (New York: William Morrow, 1990).

Joyce Carol Oates, ed., *Night Walks: A Bedside Companion* (Princeton, N.J.: Ontario Review Press, 1982).

Michael J. Thorpy and Jan Yager, *The Encyclopedia of Sleep and Sleep Disorders* (New York: Facts on File, 1991).

Acknowledgments

Thanks to the authors, agents, and publishers who kindly granted permission to reprint material from the following:

A. Alvarez, *Night,* copyright © 1995 by A. Alvarez. Reprinted by permission of W.W. Norton & Company, Inc.

A. Alvarez, *The Savage God: A Study of Suicide,* © 1990 A. Alvarez, reprinted with the permission of Gillon Aitken Associates Ltd.

Honoré de Balzac. From "Du Café," an appendix to *La Physiologie du Gout* by Jean-Anthelme Brillat-Savarin. Translation copyright © 1996 by Robert Onopa. Reprinted by permission.

Barenaked Ladies, "Who Needs Sleep," words & music by Steven Page & Ed Robertson, copyright © 1998 Reprise Records. Reprinted by permission of Warner-Chappel Music.

Samuel Beckett, *Krapp's Last Tape,* copyright © 1958 by Samuel Beckett. Used by permission of Grove/Atlantic, Inc.

Lawrence Block, *The Thief Who Couldn't Sleep,* copyright © 1966 by Lawrence Block. Reprinted with the permission of Simon & Schuster.

Jorge Luis Borges, "The Circular Ruins," from *Ficciones,* copyright © 1962 by Grove Press, Inc. Used by permission of Grove/Atlantic, Inc.

Jorge Luis Borges, "Two Forms of Insomnia," from *The Limit,* copyright © 1981 by Jorge Luis Borges, translation copyright © by Alan S. Trueblood. Reprinted with permission of The Wylie Agency, Inc.

Jean-Anthelme Brillat-Savarin, *The Philosopher in the Kitchen,* translated by Anne Drayton (Penguin Books 1970, first published as *La Physiologie du Gout,* 1825). Copyright © Anne Drayton, 1970. Reproduced by permission of Penguin Books Ltd.

Joseph Brodsky, "On Love," from *A Part of Speech,* translation copyright © 1980 by Farrar, Straus & Giroux, LLC. Reprinted by permission of Farrar, Straus & Giroux, LLC.

Picture Credits

Page 1   Magnum Photos, Inc., © Raymond Depardon
Page 3   Marcos R. Lujan
Page 8   Jeffrey Newberry
Page 16   David Graham
Page 20   Jerry N. Uelsmann, *Untitled*, © 1963
Pages 22–3   © Kaz
Page 24   Courtesy of Jerry Ohlinger
Page 27   Brad Pitt in *Johnny Suede*, courtesy of Jerry Ohlinger
Page 28   *Dracula's Daughter*, courtesy of Everett Collection
Page 31   J. E. Lecadre, *Untitled,* c. 1871–96, albumen print
Page 35   Marcos R. Lujan
Page 38   *Beauty and the Beast*, courtesy of Jerry Ohlinger
Page 40   Poster for *White Zombie,* courtesy of Everett Collection, Inc.
Page 44   Arthur Tress
Page 50   Courtesy of Jerry Ohlinger
Page 53   *Night of the Living Dead*, courtesy of Everett Collection, Inc.
Page 55   Daniel Furon
Page 57   *It Happened One Night*, courtesy of Everett Collection, Inc.
Page 60   *Young Frankenstein*, courtesy of Jerry Ohlinger
Page 62   Marcos R. Lujan
Page 67   Daniel Furon
Page 71   Brett Panelli
Page 72   The Kobal Collection
Page 76   Masatoshi Nagase
Page 79   Magnum Photos, Inc., © Erich Hartmann
Page 82   Jeffrey Newberry
Page 88   From *The Best of Lewis Carroll*
Page 90   © Peter Kuper
Page 100   Magnum Photos, Inc., © Larry Towell
Page 106   From the collections of the Library of Congress
Pages 112–3   Courtesy of Jerry Ohlinger
Page 114   *Only Two Can Play*, 1962, The Kobal Collection
Page 120   The Kobal Collection
Page 123   Marilyn Monroe in *Some Like it Hot*, courtesy of Jerry Ohlinger
Page 126   Jeffrey Newberty
Page 138   Courtesy of Jerry Ohlinger
Page 143   Jerry Lewis and Renee Taylor in *Errand Boy*, 1961, Everett Collection, Inc.
Page 144   William Hurt in *Altered States*, courtesy Everett Collection, Inc.
Page 151   Courtesy of Jerry Ohlinger
Page 152   Angela Wyant
Page 157   William Parker Little, *Under the Arc Lights, Columbus, OH—1905*, from the Paul Hooge collection

Page 158   Thomas Ott, *Greetings from Hellville*
Page 163   Courtesy of Jerry Ohlinger
Page 164   Magnum Photos, Inc., © Donovan Wylie
Page 169   Doris Day and Richard Widmark in *The Tunnel of Love*, 1958, The Kobal Collection
Page 170   Amy Robinson and Harvey Keitel in *Mean Streets*, Photofest
Page 174   Robert Ryan in *Crossfire*, Photofest
Page 177   *Smash-Up*, Photofest
Page 180   Thomas Ott, *Greetings from Hellville*
Page 188   From *The Best of Lewis Carroll*
Page 190   *Medea* (oil on panel), Anthony Frederick Augustus Sandys (1829–1904),
            Birmingham Museums and Art Gallery/Bridgeman Art Library
Page 197   Gustave Doré
Page 199   *Shock Treatment*, Everett Collection, Inc.
Page 200   *Snow White*, Everett Collection, Inc.
Page 205   Courtesy of Jerry Ohlinger
Page 207   *Some Like it Hot*, courtesy of Jerry Ohlinger
Page 208   *Forest Gump*, Photofest
Page 216   The Original Three Stooges in *Stop! Look! And Laugh!* Everett Collection
Page 217   The Everett Collection; *The Cradle*, 1872, by Berthe Morisot (1841–95),
            Musee d'Orsay, Paris, France/Peter Willi/Bridgeman Art Library
Page 220   Courtesy of the Neal Peters Collection
Page 221   Thomas Ott, *Greetings from Hellville*
Page 222   © Kaz
Page 225   *Talk of the Town*, The Kobal Collection
Pages 230–1 Sukita

About the Authors

Deborah Bishop lives in San Francisco, where she writes for a variety of publications. She is a graduate of UC Berkeley in English Literature. Her first bout of insomnia occurred in nursery school, when she found her mind wandering during naptime. She shares a bed with her husband, Michael, and cat, Stella—both champion sleepers.

David Asher Levy is a partner in Thirsty Eye, a creative services agency in New York. He has twice been a finalist for the Nicholl Fellowships in Screenwriting, sponsored by the Academy of Motion Picture Arts and Sciences. He briefly attended the Yale School of Drama, and his five plays have been produced on stages from Los Angeles to New York. He sleeps a lot, and enjoys it.

About the Designer

Roger Gorman is the principal and creative director of Reiner Design Consultants, New York. He has received design awards from the Art Director's clubs of New York and Los Angeles, the Society of Publication Designers, the American Institute of Graphic Arts and Print, as well as a 1990 Grammy for his design of David Bowie's "Sound & Vision." Despite all his successes, Roger Gorman is a tortured soul and drinks himself to sleep each night.